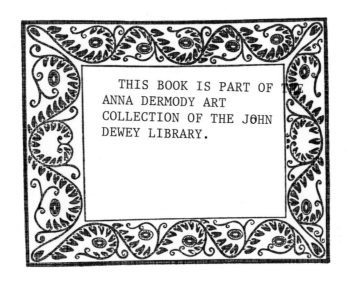

RICHARD NEUTRA

BUILDING WITH NATURE

UNIVERSE BOOKS

NEW YORK

Published in the United States of America in 1971 by Universe Books, 381 Park Avenue South,
New York, N.Y. 10016
© Verlagsanstalt Alexander Koch GmbH, Stuttgart
Library of Congress Catalog Card Number: 79-93953
ISBN 0-87663-133-2
Printed in Germany

CONTENTS

FOREWORD

The German edition of this book, published early in 1970 by Verlagsanstalt Alexander Koch of Stuttgart, was dedicated to my parents' long friendship and admiration for Frank Lloyd Wright, the one hundredth anniversary of whose birth was marked in 1969. This edition should properly memorialize my father, whose death on April 16, 1970 followed by only a week the celebration of his seventy-eighth birthday. A week later, the United States celebrated the first Earth Day, a nationwide observance of the importance of ecology to man's survival.

At the beginning of 1970, my father was at the zenith of his career and creative abilities, and although his doctors had often warned him about overexertion and excitement, he continued to work and live at the same frenzied pace he had for nearly half a century. When he and my mother left for a three-week tour of Europe in early April—he was the keynote speaker at an international conference on bathing establishments in Sindelfingen—we were just in the beginning stages of a number of important projects.

On April 16, in the late afternoon, I received a long-distance telephone call from Wuppertal, in which I was curtly informed that my father had just died of a heart attack after two days of strenuous photography of two houses.

For the nearly thirty years that I had been associated with my father in the planning of projects such as are illustrated in this book, he had often spoken of his death and of the heritage he would be leaving me and others who were like-minded as the collaborators then involved in the planning of these houses. (See page 223.) A good many times during those years, his health and state of mind had been such that those close to him were genuinely concerned for his survival. That he departed from us in this way, especially so far from home, was a shock, not because it had not been anticipated but because at this particular time he seemed so vital, alive, sparkling, and even more energetic than at times in the near past. As my mother said, "He was a Sunday child." She meant that even in death he managed not to be a burden to anyone and to leave us all with a memory of great vitality and energy, those qualities that characterized his life.

My mother and I take comfort in the fact that my father was aware of the rising public concern for problems that he had been discussing at least a generation earlier. He lived to see the public recognition of these ideals and their dedication by public observance of concern for these matters on a nationwide basis. Plans for an Ecology Park have been unveiled, the inspiration for which came to me, on Earth Day 1970, when I thought how Richard Neutra might himself have wished to be memorialized. The idea was to provide a Contemplation Park, consisting only of a beautifully landscaped space, complete with nature's green and water, in which a person could remove himself for a moment from the rush of everyday life and contemplate the importance of nature in man's scheme of things. Here might be displayed some of the statements made by Neutra and others who pioneered in recognizing the importance of nature to man's constructed environment.

Although this book will be one of the last containing original writings by my father and therefore it is fitting that it memorialize him, my mother, my brother Raymond, and I are working on several other manuscripts in various stages of completion, and they will be ready for publication soon. The fact that I worked on many of the projects pictured here and that clients can still look to our office for similar kinds of environments makes us hope that more such publications will feature the Neutra oeuvre, as my father had lately referred to it.

The rebuilt Research House, so richly pictured in this volume, has special significance to me, since I was awakened at midnight in late March 1963 by a telephone call announcing that the family home was on fire. I got dressed and rushed to the scene—my parents were away from the city—and tried to convince the firemen to save certain important material by breaking second-floor windows and directing the hose streams to keep down the heat. The building was so badly damaged that it had to be demolished down to the original foundation.

During the next three years, I found myself principally responsible for the replanning and negotiation with authorities to permit the rebuilding of the structure in the original spirit. My parents were absent for long periods during the reconstruction, although we were in correspondence and contact about every detail.

The cover photograph has sentimental importance to me, since my second marriage occurred on the roof during the roof framing stage underneath the tree in the background. During the two years of construction that followed, my new family and I lived in the garden house to the rear of the site, and we supervised the construction on a daily basis. It was here that we had many of our discussions about the means available to the architect for expansion of space by means of design techniques rather than only by square footage.

In 1930, when my father first began planning the original Research House, it was his purpose to demonstrate how space could be utilized on a small urban lot. At the same time, the appearance of the building represented a vast departure from what was common at that time. (Imagine the Spanish-style houses and vintage automobiles that were being produced in that year!) When we started the reconstruction with the constraints placed upon us, it was clear that the style of the architecture would not be as revolutionary as it had been thirty-odd years earlier, but the space concepts were still as fresh and could be further expanded. For this reason, we introduced the use of reflective surfaces, in the form of water, glasses, and mirrors of varying densities, to experiment with these possibilities. The rebuilt Research House is an enrichment and expansion of the original concepts of a generation ago.

The fact that we were able, with complete ease, to rebuild the family home following the same general design philosophy thirty-five years after its first construction demonstrates the deep-seated conviction that structures to house man have a much more basic origin than current

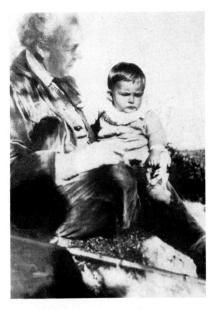

As a token of devotion to their great friend Frank Lloyd Wright, Richard and Dione Neutra called their first son Frank L. Neutra. He often sat on his namesake's lap in Taliesin.

style. This is amply illustrated by the quantity of projects in this volume, all of which have a certain affinity that unifies them in a continuum and makes them universally attractive to man the world over, regardless of race, creed, or national origin.

It was our theory that the physical design of man's habitation should spring from his "original equipment"—namely, his sensory perception apparatus—and from his common origin in the mild climatic region of the Central African equatorial zone. No matter how far he wanders north or south of the equator, man has always retained his affinity for nature, and it has been our goal to bring him ever closer thereto, by whatever technological means at our disposal. In this way, even in harsh and unfriendly climates, by the use of double glazing, heating, electrification, and other devices, we are able to make the outside available to man the year round.

Although the individual residence did not form a major part of our work during the past twenty-odd years, my father and I had felt that it was here that the most basic encounter with man occurred and where intimate discussions could be undertaken with individual members of a family who would personally be touched by what was designed. With the design of such structures as are here illustrated, we learned the most subtle lessons about human scale and reaction to the environment that could be applied also to larger public buildings, which can so easily tend to be inhuman in scale.

Rather than dwell on the technical details usually found in books on architecture, the photographs selected for inclusion here attempt to convey some of the subtle effects and exhilaration of the interplay of nature and architecture through the maximum use of transparency and indoor-outdoor living.

I know that my father hoped to pass on the results of some of our efforts to demonstrate the ability of modern technology to permit man to move ever closer to nature. This, coupled with the respect for the site and its inherent beauties wherever it might be, will form a heritage to be treasured and further developed for the future.

It was one of my father's last wishes that the Los Angeles organization of the Neutra Institutes be renamed the Institute for Survival Through Design, so that it would have broader appeal to everyone who might be inclined to work toward the goals for which it was formed. The major aims and purposes of the Institute are to foster interdisciplinary research between the design professions and related specialists in the natural, behavioral, and other sciences whose information should be evermore used in the planning of the environment as well as in the education of an enlightened consumership to more effectively judge the design results; to make available the accumulated knowledge being developed in the field to those engaged in the planning of the environment; and to publish case histories of actual experiences in design, which would be of value to the design professions.

My father always regarded our practice as a mission rather than a business. I share his view and pledge to carry on the tradition of building with nature and producing a lasting value for our clients which transcends the particular fashion which happens to be in vogue at any given moment. It is my sincere desire to encourage continued research and the dissemination of its results, as well as to produce further works demonstrating concern for the effect of designed environments on the people who inhabit them. As my father often said, "Man—in the middle—is the measure." May our physical structures consider man first!

Dion Neutra
Los Angeles, California
July 30, 1970

THE INDIVIDUAL COUNTS—BUILDING MUST LASTINGLY SERVE HIM

Marcus Tullius Cicero owned well-paying but otherwise highly dubious multistoried apartments in Rome. They were called "insulae," perhaps because in them, especially on the higher floors, one was cut off from escape whenever a fire (which occurred frequently) threatened one of those densely occupied, monstrous buildings. Here it was that Cicero had a profitable business, but not when he was declaiming his remarkably constructed speeches against Catiline in the Senate. In Rome, business was called "negotium," meaning "absence of leisure," and "procul negotiis" was the typical expression for "far from work." Marcus Tullius Cicero also had a villa in the country, far from work, for his leisure hours—the still famous Tusculum.

Tusculum and the "insulae" represent the extreme ends of the Roman architectural spectrum. They depict how far one can go in disposing of one's own time and space. It is frightening to what extremes the massing together of human life can be carried on in certain circumstances. The military, the victorious Roman legions, were lodged in barracks that were even more cramped than the miserable apartments of most Roman citizens.

In spite of the congestion of golden ages—those of Augustus in Rome and of Bismarck in Berlin, for example—after wars have been won and attempts have been made to make the people happy and show calculated respect for massed-together humanity, there are still, in many places, instructive, salutary remnants of individual habitats. That is still possible, even if everything round about is rashly "decreed"; and, in future, such houses must be brought together with more foresight.

Old and new villas—today's Tusculums—still exist: in the Sachsenwald or farther down the Elbe River in Hamburg; dachas near Moscow; and ministers' holiday retreats along the Bulgarian coast. In such places, people try to order their space and time somewhat more loosely than they are disposed of by others around them.

One questions whether the trend toward erecting multistoried condominiums in Chicago, in São Paulo, or even in socialist Sofia and Brno, will cause the private dwelling to fall irrevocably into oblivion. After all, much depends on very human responses and is influenced in the most natural way. Hence, the personal conduct of the future resident makes itself felt: He can be happy when enjoying a warm and trusting relationship with his advisor—an architect capable of enthusiasm. The architect, for his part, while in a dicussion with his clients, is in a far better position if he can turn to animated human faces.

Few young people study architecture merely to replace mass data-processing machines. In order to program such machines or, even better, to head a department of the prefabricating industry, an architect needs at the outset at least some individual contact and personal experience.

The enthusiastic student of architecture does not want to be considered an imitator even when he is one. He sees himself as an individually creative handler of human problems. From the very beginning of my professional work, in all modesty, I wanted to feel somewhat like a foreman and creator of prototypes. From such endeavor, I later derived such standards as the "tradition analog" of our time. But it was always recognizable, living individuals who went into the laboratory of my youthful research and practice of milieu-molding and whom I examined with empathy, in terms of their past and future. Such individual experiences lead the clinician—as they led me—to diverse but also to repeated, deepened insights.

A pedagogue who never sees the charges entrusted to him would be as ridiculous an oddity as a doctor who un-Hippocratically does not see his patients face to face. He can see them with his own eyes, even in the largest polyclinic. No doctor would voluntarily do without all physiognomic contacts and impressions—without the so-called human relationships. Sometimes, in a flash, these cast more light on the psychosomatic ailments than do detailed laboratory findings.

It is also clear, however, that the observer modifies the observed. Students confront the experienced pedagogue with certain already existing inferiority feelings. The doctor deals mainly with depressed people, who come, so to say, to beg for their lives. These people are comparatively so much easier to lead and serve, as they are called from classrooms or to clinic waiting rooms before the impressive examiner, than those whom the architect wants to assist.

In German, the architect's clients are called "Bauherren," a title well suited to Louis XIV and Frederick the Great, who approached their self-willed building duties with brilliant optimism and who quite possibly knew how to finance them with a predatory war or two. But the feudal age is gone for good. The experiences with a family group of cohabitators (symbiotics), with their single dwelling, have provided the architect valuable revelations up to this time.

Even on a restricted scale, the fantastic new methods and means offer us more than Marie Antoinette could experience in her chateau, or in milkmaid's garb in the sentimental section of her grandiose park.

When, as occasion would have it, a young man telephones an architect, as his prospective client, he naturally does not proceed as if he were entering the treatment room from a doctor's waiting room full of the more or less depressed. Rather, he regards himself as happy and at the beginning of a career, feels he is betrothed for life to the most charming girl and that he can expect a considerable salary raise at the first of the year which will allow him to go into debt for thirty years. Descendant of the capitalist of former times, he does not want to feel deprived in a mass of consumers. He blissfully overrates the loan the banker will give him, in order to raise his future children in the best manner in a milieu open to vital elements. Really, a man who looks into the farthest future with such inexpressible assurance is more than just an optimist. There is something maniacal about him! People in a manic phase feel entitled to a very different kind of treatment and are open to another kind of advice than those who beg for their lives.

The meeting between the architect and client does not have the character of a gloomy enumeration of depressing symptoms and a fearful kind of hope. Instead, it begins with a felicitous discourse, supported perhaps by confessions, but all of them accentuated by the cheerful viewing of what is to come. The architect does not sit there with a serious face like a medical man but is rather carefree at first, with a friendly smile and with eyes that already show many rays of hope.

When he has a chance to prepare the case better, by letter or long-distance telephone call, he questions the client, who already desires an individual habitat yet with the anticipation that he is not simply a single person. No one ever builds "in vacuo" for himself alone and without other consequences. Always a group of clients is involved: Even if the man regards himself as a confirmed bachelor, he is not simply and wholly without relatives. Rather, he is, in most cases, happily married, has or expects children, and has, as well, expectations about how he or his wife, or both, will raise the children.

A doctor who is not a charlatan would never make promises beyond his own generation. The architect, however, is a magician who at least vaguely promises much that reaches into the distant future—a happiness that endures until all is paid off in thirty years (and longer still, if at all possible). That the magic can really last a lifetime has been shown to me truly gratifyingly by many letters and by my subsequent visits to the environments I had molded.

Whenever the architect has prepared everything fully, he has also comprehended in terms of a warning, however, that according to his experience—and this has truly been my experience throughout half a century—people do not marry each other because they are identical but precisely because they are not, because they complement each other. The conclusion, then, is that both partners in marriage do not have an identical make-up and that one always makes himself more heard than the other. In a meeting with the architect, one partner will always be heard somewhat more than the other. But being heard less does not always mean being less important or less decisive!

In any event, I have found, and have for a long time suggested, that those involved in a house-building project should first be consulted, each in seclusion, undisconcerted and unadvised by others, and encouraged to unburden their wishful hearts on paper without anyone looking over their shoulder, in order to avoid, or at least to lessen, years of friction later on.

We now come to the stage that the doctor would call the examination and that follows the spontaneous, subjective report of the patient about the previous history of his case. The doctor completes this report through additional questions, which may be dry and objective. But no patient resents this, and it does not cool the developing relationship of trust. An architect who, so to speak, sets about making a prognosis for a lifetime cannot send his client to the dressing room! He cannot even ask point-blank questions about very intimate things, even on the subject of the time-honored middle-class milieu with its capital reserves, income, or the chances of an inheritance.

But the "anamnesis"—the most open memory-report about the purely physiological—is very much hindered here. For the architect cannot even touch upon, through direct questions, the highly important biologically determinative circumstances of those who wish to entrust themselves to him. If, for example, he must know the predominant sensual sensitivities of Mr. Smith, as he sits before him, he had better do this somewhat casually and with a bit of humor. He may perhaps ask, "When you come home and turn the key of the front door, Mr. Smith, how many steps do you want to take before you smell that your wife is cooking cauliflower or sauerkraut for supper again tonight?" The answer in one case (let us say Mr. Smith's) is also casual. He smiles, as if he were taking the matter as a joke. But in another case (with Mr. Brown, perhaps), the face darkens in a lightning flash. He speaks indignantly and with extreme repugnance of this sort of trouble, which has spoiled his mood for years—especially when he enters the house from the garage by the service entrance and already smells the foul air instead of being allowed to experience a happier homecoming.

During such statements by one marriage partner, the architect always closely observes the facial expression of the other. He may notice that the wife finds this outburst slightly ridiculous and exaggerated. Silently, the architect notes: "Mrs. B.—'olfactorily minus'—much less endowed by nature, and also evidently less plagued than Mr. Brown, with nose problems." With this, he has gained a general, highly important insight, with implications that go far beyond the Brown case at hand.

The senses can indeed disturb life to an extreme. Something like one marriage partner's sensitivity to smell, which the milieu-molder notes briefly here like a diagnostician, can mean "cumulative," ever-increasing, and even extreme irritation for decades of married life. Take, for instance, "He won't stop smoking in the bedroom, no matter how I plead with him!" The complaint really sounds emotionally emphatic. One can be just as emphatic about the practical pass-through counter connecting directly with the dining room, with its attendant cooking vapor, about which one person is more solicitous than the other. The era of scientifically developed ventilation will come one day. At least preparatory measures now will later save values from premature aging. The situation is similar when the architect discusses a kitchen table surface made of tile, stainless steel, or plastic laminate, where in each case the chaotic clatter of the plates and silverware reaches various degrees of noise. Sometimes there even ensues an emotional outburst on the part of one or the other person, from which the architect again quickly draws his conclusions, this time about auditive disposition.

The varying sensitivities to noise would give him reason to immediately consider, for instance, the positioning of the noisy television set within this family group, regardless of how the turning down of the volume is tolerated by the various people concerned.

In none of these cases—whether it concerns the orientation of the bedroom toward the bright sunrise or one partner's night reading habits in bed—do laboratory tests ever seem permitted or expected, while people let themselves be attended by an architect for so many years to come. Such tests would be extremely useful, in order to complement the doctor's examination with scientific carefulness.

Naturally, as I said, it is out of the question for the architect to have even a chance of casting a glance at the doubtless informative anatomy of his charges, from which a good judge of people like old Hippocrates was always able to conclude so much. The diagnosis, which is briefly formulated by the doctor in Latin, is here considered by the architect more vaguely, and in silence; and all that is discussed is the therapeutic side, which he somehow emphasizes in his solution and expresses in a convincing, rather persuasive manner. There is no one-word proclamation about the patient's condition, as in the case of a doctor who believes he has recognized a suffering and names it. No one really wants to hear from the architect that his case is typical—that would really be justifiably against his feeling of individuality—nor does he want to hear that his condition might allow anything like a dubious prognosis.

The good architect does not disturb his client by shaking his head or by mentioning too many of the vicissitudes of life or by letting them crop up in conversation. But through honest assumption of the client's trust, he becomes his friend, so that, in spite of all the newspaper or magazine clippings shown to him during the talk, he can protect whoever has entrusted himself to him even somewhat against the person's will. But it is never a matter of argument. I can hardly remember a single one in half a century. Here much more is involved than victory.

In American usage, an inalienable acquisition, a large investment that cannot be liquidated, is called a "white elephant." White elephants, though very conspicuous indeed, are not saleable in South Asia and they have no market value. Both the exotic and the fashion of the day are two poles of unfunctional decision-making. Either through pure extraordinariness or through purely conformist fashion-madness, they possess a value that in the long run is not generally human or redeemable.

And it is precisely with this idea that Adolf Loos influenced me more than half a century ago, by the Danube, long before I began to work by the Pacific Ocean. From him I won the conviction that we have the dependable yardstick of an architect's accomplishment in durable value and timelessness, quite apart from the one-night triumph of the best hairdresser or the seasonal business of ladies' apparel. After all, we want some "change" in such things; but the prettiest hat that my dear wife ever bought we paid for right on the spot, over the counter, and didn't have to pay off over decades, until our golden wedding anniversary. On the other hand, I feel happy to have many witnesses who found that what I built long ago remained dear not only to the parents and the long-since-grown-up children as a meeting place for the family but that its value rose much more than even the price of the land. And that means a lot in the American real estate market, where much that is used often undergoes the opposite of a rise in value over a few years' time.

I remember a humorous little incident with Adolf Loos, who could produce such a friendly-wicked smile. It no doubt influenced me unforgettably for life. (As his wife writes, he also gladly remembered me to the end.) For a long time he had opposed a highly successful contemporary who later directed a great government-supported art academy in Vienna. Loos always grinned and ironically called him The Professor. I remember how Loos entered his "American Bar" one evening when we young people were awaiting him. (By the way, I revisited this Viennese bar after fifty-five years, and it is unchanged, quite extraordinarily, so that the little story of long ago now becomes doubly significant.) Loos approached us, and immediately began to recount: "I have just seen The Professor in the Cafe Museum. As I passed by his table, where he was sitting with a few bigwigs, I said, 'I rode by this afternoon on the streetcar past one of your houses.' 'Where? Which one was it?' 'On such and such a street,' I said, Whereupon The Professor made a wry face. 'Don't look at it! I built it three years ago!' To which I said very quietly, 'You see? That's the difference between you and me. Now you say it's trash; I said that already three years ago!'" I still see and feel how Loos could flash a smile and teach enduringly.

Intense technical activity surrounds the Research House, which was originally built in Los Angeles around 1930. The city increased its population and industry sixfold within the richly constructive lifetime of Richard Neutra. Los Angeles grew as a "dependent" of Detroit, the first automobile city, whose conveyor belts roll cars into the entire world. It offered the best, winterless, snow- and ice-free climate in all the world, and this ideal atmosphere soon became more and more densely impregnated with exhaust fumes. But even internal combustion engines, like everything else not sifted and developed with the harmful side effects of technology in mind, must be transitory in the long run. Neutra confidently hoped

that technology itself is neutral. It can just as easily take a positive turn, when bio-realism * is applied with understanding and when careful choices, based on an abundance of research results, are made for human milieu-molding.

In these downtown confines, and on remote exotic sites all over the world, the architect can build houses large and small, with modern technological means. They will gain in spaciousness when they find an intimate bond with nature

* Neutra defined biorealism as follows: Bios, the Greek word for life, comprises the infinitely manifold emotive powers of our self. The word real refers to life-reality and steers away from vague abstractions.

The Research House, seat of the Neutra Institute, renamed the Institute for Survival Through Design in honor of Neutra's book, has been known for almost forty years as a research center at Silver Lake. Light, such as the glass areas reflecting the heat radiation waves of a southern exposure, overpowers neighboring disturbances within the field of vision. Reflected images from a "roof pond" seem to lend to the roof level of the Research House a free, pleasant relationship to the surroundings, in the midst of metropolitan Los Angeles. The living, changing reflections perceived by the eye are again frozen by the optical tricks of the camera. Even here, the photograph can only partially select from the sensual continuum.

Mirrored on the water terrace, in their refreshing, nature-related appearance, is an arrangement of potted plants.

The view toward the morning sky behind the trees of the small property reveals, above the water-roof terrace, the heat- and light-reflecting east and south front of the penthouse. To the right, at eye level, under the trellised framework for climbing plants, is another half-reflecting glass screen. This might perhaps appear confining if seen from a neighbor's place, but actually, it carefully screens the light and thus not only beautifies the space visually and effectively but also seems to expand it.

Above the water roof of the Neutra Institute, one sees the tops of trees that were planted as a visual screen at the nearby property line to the north.

Sliding doors open to a roof terrace still farther in the foreground (not seen here) and to the shallow water, into which one can place, as desired, some stepping stones or flower pots. At night, when they are illuminated by the mild white moonlight, they seem even more to reveal the surrounding nature to the resident and the visitor.

Water, this time on the garage roof, reflects a spiral staircase and the foliage of
a eucalyptus tree, which manages to find
room for its roots on this small property
(63 × 71 feet).

On the balcony terrace of the southern living room, water replaces a railing, which would intrusively hem in the view, and while the protective water boundary gently ripples with the breeze, it pleasantly emphasizes the natural view and dramatizes the foreground.

The water reservoir in the center of the continually growing city of millions, Los Angeles. To the right of Silverlake, behind the trees, are the headquarters of the Neutra Institute, now raised to the rank of a historic monument, which its founders named after half a century of pioneering work. In the foggy background visible here, Neutra, by order of the city, had leveled one of the highest mountain ridges and made preparations for an enchanting convalescent center project, which, like many of his best designs, did not reach the stage of execution.

The terraces of the roof garden under the trellis afford a panoramic view of Silverlake, whose waters, visually fused with the foreground water surface, unite in an impression of wide space.

The exhaust gases of the heaviest traffic in the world have made the northern mountain chains, upon which the Pacific Ocean breezes break, disappear ever more into smog since the time that Neutra erected his Research House on the bank of the dark lake more than a generation ago. He wanted to show how the often senseless expansion of the motorized city could be better renewed in close relation to nature—that nearness to nature so beneficial for the vitality of its millions of inhabitants.

Experience Gained from the Research House

Our living space should not be separated too much or too long from the green world of the organic! The immense foliage masses of the tropical jungle do not oppress us, as would the arid inorganic foreign properties of a moon landscape or an area in downtown Manhattan. These rigid volumes, towering and stretching solidly or twisting in monumental curves, are attractive in photographs. In reality, we find them disproportionate compared with our small but living corporeality, which seems lost in that future metropolis united in a single super-structure which I myself have often proposed. But we must articulate this large-scale communal habitation into a multiplicity of better proportioned, "greened-over" corners, balconies, and water terraces, webbing even the starkly patched concrete slabs with growing vegetation.

Hydroponics seems to me to be a promising new technique whereby nutritive substances dissolved in water, perhaps even heated in winter, would be pumped upward from a carefully serviced central location. The fluid would flow into the receptacles of flower windows on many stories, and would support hanging gardens and roof terraces without the need for the services of a swarming army of plant tenders. One could "green over" the highest massive building structures with striking varieties of ivy, for instance, like a two-storied Oxford college in former times.

Into the most well-proportioned room of the building we are in we carry with us a lively, though subconscious memory of the natural exterior. Barrack monotony by no means creates neighborliness within huge apartment blocks, and thus many a conducive element for it was studied in the Research House at Silverlake. Then it was also considered in all possible single-home projects in its socio-psychological effects, and later observed during residence there, including every modest bit of individualizing horticulture done about the bird cage. Even the wise, imposing masculinity of a King Solomon tends to statistical generalization, and thus "all is vanity." Is it not said of him that he had six hundred wives? Evidently it is the feminine aspect of our species that makes the mother of children so discriminating that she is able to invest even a household and dwelling place with personality.

BEWOBAU Developments in Walldorf and Quickborn *

In various parts of the United States, and in other fast-growing population centers as well, such as South Africa, South America, and South Asia, where, for years, Richard Neutra functioned as architect and planning consultant, much is being done to settle people in a new and better way. Even in Europe there are tower structures flanked by large parking lots and they are perhaps the most sensational phenomena in this aspect of living, before the whole city becomes an interwoven superstructure of fabricated giganticism. Row houses, which variously crop up in the history of American and European residential development and also have played their part in the development of the postwar era, have suffered in popularity if not in number. As early as thirty years ago, Neutra publicized patio- and atrium-houses, which shortly thereafter gained new interest in America as well as in Europe. Participating in such a housing development in the Arizona desert, Neutra studied the remains of prehistoric buildings, which show that man responds similarly in similar climatic conditions and takes measures that have a rational common denominator.

But when it comes to living, Neutra was the naturalistic architect who held the view that the rational is only a small part of the human-organic and even of the conscious. His experience in residential building extended over many decades and to a great multiplicity of clients.

"Melting pots," "community developments" exist almost everywhere today, from Johannesburg to Calcutta, and in the pine and beech forest south of the Frankfurt airport. And everything on this shrunken globe seems drawn ever closer together.

The little town of Walldorf in Germany had its first slender beginnings in 1699, when the Hessian sovereign accepted fifteen Waldensian refugee families whom Mazarin no longer wished to see in France. They founded the old town, where, with 1,500 of their descendants, a multitude of Jourdans and Cézannes live among 10,000 newcomers, including quite a number of Americans. The mayor, Mr. Zwilling (wose name means "twin"), recounts this himself: his own family's name was formerly Beson, which in older times was the French word for twin.

The rate of construction is impressive, especially in the northern part of the city and in the west along the Frankfurt-Darmstadt railway line. The surrounding forest is protected by the Darmstadt Forest Commission. The Hessian Roads Commission maintains a well-kept road at the east edge of the large forest property on which BEWOBAU (Betreuungs- und Wohnungsbaugesellschaft m. b. H., with its main office in Hamburg) is having 400 living units built. The surface area for this development comprises 350,000 square meters. This commission was carried out for the client with the greatest sympathy and devotion.

It was stimulating that the trust expressed here, over 6,000 miles away from Los Angeles, gave me a singular opportunity to place synoptically worldwide experience near Europe's largest airport. It is important to try not to jam people together or stack them up in towers but to do everything possible to plan for the coming density of future human habitat. This should be done with insight and a soulful infeeling into the given environment, actualizing all that is emotionally and biologically necessary for life. Millions of square feet of living space are being built on both sides of the "political drapery," from Detroit, Philadelphia, and Hong Kong all the way to Peking and Kiev.

Everywhere, rigid rulings and fiscal, financial-political requirements stifle the architect's stand when he is face-to-face with the client. Land and soil are leveled by bulldozers; street are measured dead-straight or are Euclidically twisted "at random," but always so that more and more cars can drive ever faster on them. America, especially, is the richest land for telegraph poles, smelling barbarically of creosote and sheltering fewer songbirds than the trees whose branches and roots were cut off before that nice leveling job began. Perhaps the pine forest has a value far beyond what all the forestry posters advertise! It is a green umbrella for airplanes flying high above the countryside—an umbrella filtering the sun. When considering the inclusion of greenery into the living space one finds the most wonderful discovery of the modern age

* From a letter written by Neutra to friends in Germany about his planning of the Walldorf community near Frankfurt. What Neutra wrote about the Walldorf project applies as well to the project he planned for Quickborn, near Hamburg.

to be the transparent enclosure of climate-controlled interiors with glass. Even the Middle Ages and the Renaissance, from Lübeck to Bremen, fell in love with the method of breaking up the exterior walls by the use of glass and went almost as far in this as the designers of the glass skyscrapers on Manhattan's Park Avenue. Sunshine is not an everyday thing, wheter in Hesse or in Schleswig. (Both are the locations of BEWO-BAU developments.)

In a forest we find mainly filtered daylight, but it contains all health factors and vitality stimulants, so that one hardly needs curtains for sun control. Nor does one need them for privacy, where, if necessary, man-high, prefabricated garden walls are put up which leave an unrestricted, refreshing view slightly upward into the conifers and beech trees. Naturally, every sunray from the southwest is happily honored by the design but, with the uncertainty of the weather, one cannot let that suffice, and rooms with wide openings onto exterior terraces become, and appear, much bigger. Gardening is restricted to certain decorative areas and of course cannot involve much work, since 27 per cent of all the women are attracted by the employment possibilities in the two nearby cities Frankfurt and Darmstadt. Employment prospects and the cost of keeping up a garden bear a definite relationship to a realistic garden size near the home.

High school teachers, government employees, graduate students, well-paid special technicians and industrial foremen, as well as district representatives of various firms, form the population that will now join Walldorf. Many trains will enable these new inhabitants (except perhaps for the older pensioners) to commute to the city. But the directors of BEWOBAU, first Mr. Tiedemann and Mr. Krüger, as well as their leading engineers, with Mr. Rebstock at the head, share the view of Mr. Flindt from Wiesbaden, who developed the real estate transactions, that German families are becoming more and more motorized, as in France, England, and especially America. The car will enable people to reach much greater employment opportunities, such as at Rüsselsheim and Opel, the Farbwerke Höchst, the Glanzstoff AG in Kelsterbach—and soon there will be half a million employees in the surrounding area.

The highway is to encroach as little as possible on the entry to and exit from the forest community. Thus, there is an entrance in the northeast, and an exit to Walldorf's water reservoir, which lends an accent of height to the landscape. Highly important, of course, is the pedestrian access to the train station, for which there is an underpass in Walldorf itself. This access leads past the local business center and the main square, as well as past the school grounds.

The irregularities of the timber stand invite welcome but not arbitrary variation, which is always more refreshing than monotonous uniformity.

In order to preserve the trees and protect the forest, the ground is not treated radically and height variations are left intact. Besides, the trees are not very large, and if heavy traffic can be prevented by the irregular layout of the streets and roads, or by slight ascents and declines, then this is exactly the plan's aim. (The greater steerability and lightness of the smaller European car give the planner means that his American colleague unfortunately does not have.) With regard to local ordinances, all the authorities were very cooperative and have begun to consider the project as a happy combination of European and American elements. One may assume that through this model community, Walldorf can gain considerable European, and even international, renown; for here the green landscape, fitted into the planning and made the measure, related to the emotions and the matrix of man's well-being in his habitat.

Two-storied dwelling, paired and grouped with single-storied houses, in glades of the Hessian forest ore nestling among groups of timber stands in the northern outskirts of Hamburg.

The plan offers sun protection on summer afternoons, privacy for windows and gardens, and spaciousness, even where property sizes must be modest.

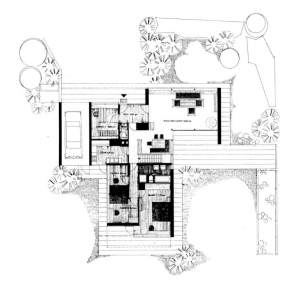

Terracing and landscape screening with fast-growing plants and evergreen shrubbery are the best provision the planner can make here. Only a few years after these preliminary photographs were taken, this development was a success, according to the enthusiastic inhabitants, who were drawn to this subdivision because of the quality of the building project. The architect arriving here from overseas was fêted spontaneously for half the night.

Walls and hedges give each of the subdivision houses a sense of seclusion.

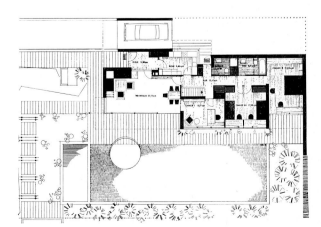

Above: The furniture, chosen by the residents themselves, seems to be interestingly influenced by a feeling for the interior layout. By now, the hedges serve their purpose—the outer rooms are now so private that the curtains are seldom drawn —and the nighttime illumination conveys to the transparent living room fronts a double worth and charm.

Center: The outdoor screening heightens the visual satisfaction of the room's extension into the outdoors.

Below: Convincing inner spaciousness of the living area; to the left, a stairway into the lower story with its children's playroom and, in some cases, with a convivial bar, which the residents installed according to the architect's models.

Right: In this small-lot colony, the architect was in some cases able to create an illusion of seclusion of houses at the edge of the forest.

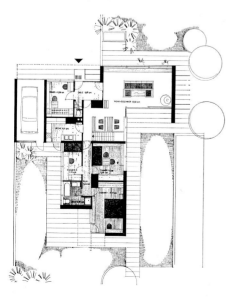

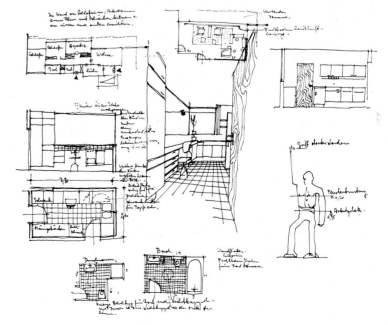

Above: Stone and natural wood contribute to the sweeping quality of the house and provide some privacy from the street. The modest masonry becomes the backdrop for the front garden.

PARISER HOUSE, UNIONTOWN, PENNSYLVANIA

Below: View from the southwest toward the entrance.

Above: An alcove bordering the kitchen provides an unadorned sitting area, which the housewife can easily survey.

Below: Stone and wood for exterior and interior are neatly fitted together, and pleasant lighting enhances the simple design.

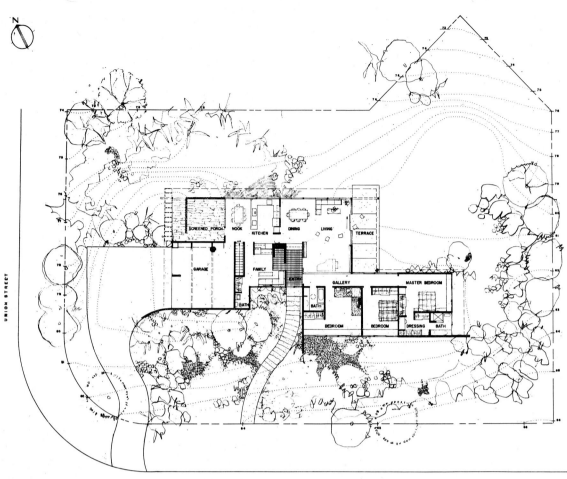

This refined house, located in Union-town, Pennsylvania, about 3,000 miles from the architect's drawing board, although somewhat hemmed in at a street corner, nevertheless enjoys a sweeping view of a broad valley. On the valley side are the living areas and the back garden. When one is looking at the landscape, the garden terrace, protected from the wind, is situated to the right of the bedroom wing. On the opposite side of the house, the delivery entrance next to the garage leads to a spacious, well-appointed kitchen with a children's counter. To the left of the entrance hall, a small den with its own fireplace rounds out the family living plan.

On entering, the visitor sees to his left a part of the library and, in front of him, something of the living room.

View from the living room toward the entrance.

The house from the south side. The wooden trellis contrasts clearly with the swimming pool.

OXLEY HOUSE, LA JOLLA, CALIFORNIA

On land overlooking the ocean, a physicist and his wife built a modest home with a master suite beyond the living areas and the studio, which form the main core of the building. The dining area, serviced from the north by a kitchen counter, opens to a patio that faces the east. The outdoor terrace overlooking the ocean to the southeast is used for social purposes. A guest room to the left of the entrance has its own circumwalled private patio. The simple building design requires little explanation, yet the architect found it especially interesting and worked at it for a long time.

This house is now the residence of Mr. and Mrs. James Darr.

Above and below: Two views from the front garden toward the small house, a white stuccoed wood-frame structure.

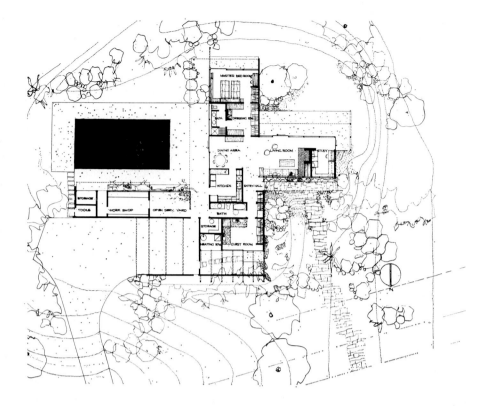

Below: View from the south.

Above: The south patio.

Below: The guest room with garden court.

TAYLOR HOUSE, GLENDALE, CALIFORNIA

A narrow builing lot can gain much by relating to an expansive view. A really unapproachable piece of mountainous land at the end of a dead-end street, between a precipitous slope and a steep precipice, is the setting for this house. It enjoys remarkable privacy and has an unimpeded view far across the San Fer- nando Valley, in the northern part of the Los Angeles area. The carport, a parking area for two cars, gives the visitor a view back toward the shrubbery on the west as he turns right to enter the house. For ease of delivery, the carport is directly connected with the kitchen. The living area, oriented to the outdoors, has

Below: View from the garden. Right: The bath opens directly into the outdoors.

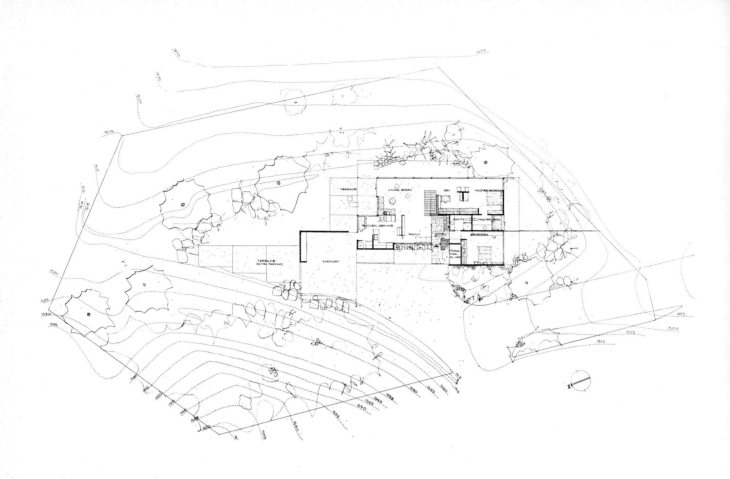

Entrance.

Above: The fireplace from the south.
Below: The fireplace from the northwest.

a main window overlooking the valley but opens onto the terrace. Adjoining the kitchen, both the exterior and the interior dining areas face west. Everything is surrounded by the silhouette of hills against the sky. Opposite, forming the east wall of the living room, the fireplace with its raised hearth and burning logs can be seen from the garden court. Farther to the east, behind the fireplace, are the sleeping quarters, with a bath that opens pleasantly onto a well-planted little courtyard.

SALE HOUSE, LOS ANGELES, CALIFORNIA

Above: View toward the living room to the distant sea, on the one side, and toward the interesting form of the nearby swimming pool, on the other.

Below: The late afternoon shadows emphasize the architectonic geometry, while the mountain forms reappear shadowlike in the glass façades.

Right: In the wind-ruffled water of the swimming pool, the calm California landscape is reflected rather more dramatically.

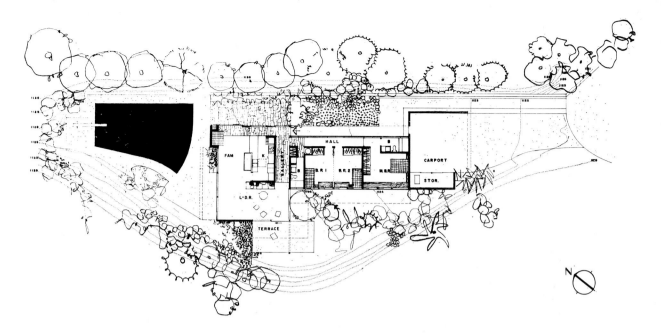

The young owners — an engineer and his artist-craftsman wife — are sensitive to natural surroundings. They wanted a modest house. The lot consisted of a rock plateau at the end of a private little street with a dramatic view over the Pacific Coast and a pleasant panorama of the countryside and a hill to the north. There the owners stroll for miles without seeing a trace of the city. The shape of the house had to fit the level and contour and be designed in relation to a swimming pool.

The entrance was planned to afford a vista, opposite the façades. From this originated a gallery with overhead lighting for the owner's small works of art, supplemented suitably by electric lighting. The living room and bedrooms have a dramatic view of the Pacific, and

The terraces and the living room are unified, perceptually blending interior and exterior.

View from the living room through the glass wall to the swimming pool and a reflection of the landscape.

a bedroom mirror extending to the windows reflects the city lights in the evening. The family room and kitchen open to a wind-sheltered, screened terrace, adjacent to the swimming pool, where a picnic table can be placed without detracting from the view of the distant landscape. A second bath, reached from the swimming pool's flagstone apron, lessens the amount of housework and makes unnecessary any other changing rooms at the pool.

The installation of stippled acoustic ceilings in the entertaining area necessitated an increase in ceiling height by 1 foot. The outside walls of this area, insulated with additional wood sheathing, created a pavilion effect desired by the owners. Since the property was too confined for future building expansion, the foundations of the carport were planned for a possible second story. A tile wall separating the main bath and the exhibition gallery was planned for mosaics designed by the owner's wife.

The interestingly designed illumination gives the house constantly changing qualities of light depending on the time of day. Oriented to the north and south, the eaves have at their edge continuous illumination (as often occurs in Neutra's designs) which lights not only the interior rooms but also the outside garden. In the gallery, overhead strip lighting is used. A light strip extending under the hall windows as far as the bath illuminates the plaster ceiling and lends a warm light to the entrance at the opposite end of this wall. In addition, various outlets provide for experimental garden illumination, to do justice to the evolving vegetation in the future as well.

A large mirror heightens the effectiveness of the mosaic and doubles the size of the room.

CYTRON HOUSE, BENEDICT CANYON, BEVERLY HILLS, CALIFORNIA

An elderly couple acquired a lot facing a deep valley road with a very restricted level or buildable area, beyond a creek's cut-in bed and steeply rising land behind, to the setting sun. The main and wonderful feature of this piece of land was and remained a colossal aged sycamore tree, with a formidable trunk rooted between road and creek which it overshadows with low, far-reaching branches. The house has its drive-in bridge over the creek at the northerly end of the frontage. At the southeast corner, a zig-zagging path sinks and, after passing under the tree and over the wide timber-constructed bridge, again rises to the visitor's entrance, giving the illusion of much more open land than exists. A reflecting pool, dammed up under the bridge, adds by day and at night with its illuminated mirroring of the mighty tree to the illusion of idyllic seclusion. The house with bedroom wing, including a little artist's studio for the lady of the house in a right angle to the street at

Above left: View from the side of the vegetation-covered hill onto the low house. The living room and master bedroom open onto the garden by means of a sliding glass door. In the evenings, from the bed, one can see opossums and raccoons which come to be fed. Even deer come down from the mountains. The elderly retired couple constantly enjoy observing these wild creatures.

Below left: Leading to the low-set- modest home is a bridge crossing a watercourse, which the architect transformed into a reflecting pond.

Above: View from the entrance through the large window of the painter's studio and toward the trees.

Below: Detail of the studio; to the right, the watercourse under the bridge, with a sycamore tree towering above. This huge tree, the largest display piece that this property offers, was lovingly included in the composition.

This photograph shows the watercourse in the foreground and the studio to the left.

left, and living quarters parallel with the street in front and mountain barriers in back, expands naturally and openly into the garden. There is an informally circumplanted area higher up, overlooking the terrace-like roof and the imposing lacy tree against the mountain silhouette across the narrow valley.

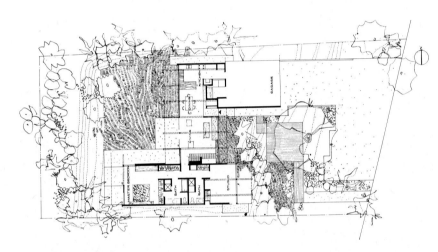

View through the living room, with its vinyl cork floor, toward the fireplace and one of the owner's works of art. The fireplace alcove with bench has sectional shelves and a dark brown leather couch.

View from the fireplace toward the entrance, which is hidden by a clothes closet. In the background, the kitchen can be seen behind the sitting area.

Below: View from the kitchen toward a cupboard with built-in bar, where the owners, while breakfasting, can see through the window their "wild visitors" in the garden.

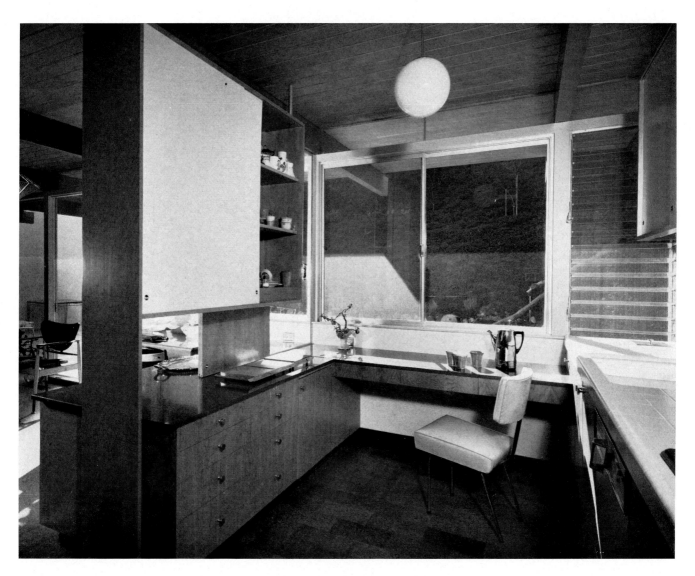

HOUSE IN BRYN ATHEN, PENNSYLVANIA

Situated in expansive and densely wooded hill country, the house overlooks a deep, idyllic valley and serves a family hoping to be richly blessed with children. In the Swedenborg community of Bryn Athen, to which the residents belong, religious meetings often take place in the home. From the entrance door, an interestingly reflective stairway ascends to an art gallery. From there, on the one side, one reaches the living room, which opens on both fronts into the outdoors, where there is a large balcony-terrace with a valley vista; adjacent are the library and the master bedroom with the bath facing the garden.

On the opposite side is the guest room, which can also be reached from the servants' quarters and kitchen. Adjoining the kitchen is the dining room, which is centrally located between the living area and the playroom, near the children's bedrooms. It is graced by an illuminated aquarium, which separates it from the sunken living room without disturbing spatial qualities.

Left: The concrete, stucco, and wood exterior is completely protected against the dampness, freezing temperatures, and accumulation of snow that are characteristic of this region.

Above: The main façade, opened wide into the shady woods, reflects in its plate glass the foliage at the edge of the broad canyon, where the Swedenborgian community of Bryn Athen was built over the course of decades. The guest room wing commands a view of splendid trees, the idyllic valley stretching below and toward the distant hills.

Center: The southwest ascent from the garden.

Below: The back entrance of the house is often used by the family. It, too, has a scenically attractive placement and is enhanced in summer with greenery. In the foreground is the southerly roof-terrace, and, to the right, the wing consisting of the children's rooms.

The stairway ascent.

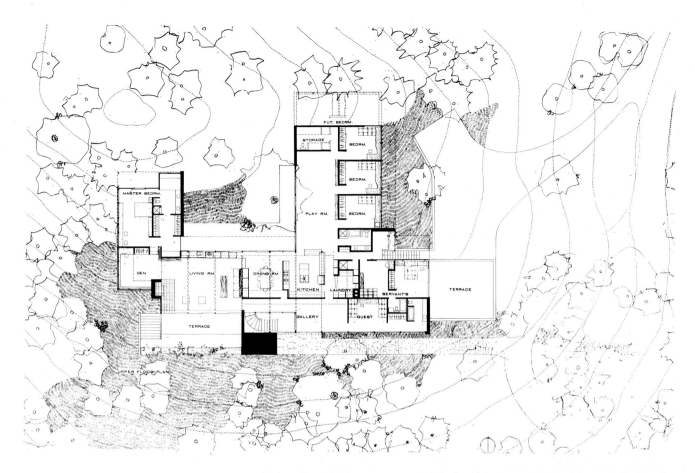

UPPER FLOOR PLAN

View toward the fireplace and the simple bronze chest, from which the Swedenborgian family takes the honored folio Bible when they assist at religious gatherings in their home.

Entrance stairs and art gallery.

The dining room with a view toward the dark trusses.

Westward view toward fireplace and in right background.

The illuminated aquarium divides the higher dining area level from the slightly sunken living quarters.

Above left: The children's dining area and southward view into the kitchen.

Above: right: View from living room toward dining room, kitchen, and the garden outside the children's playroom.

Below: View from the kitchen northward into the snowy garden and the children's playroom, which in summer can be opened widely to the outdoors.

Above left: The lawn court, looking toward the parents' wing.

Above right: A toddler bathes in the terrazzo pool.

Below: Warm air sweeps over the high glass front. This woodland site affords complete privacy.

OHARA HOUSE, LOS ANGELES, CALIFORNIA

On Argent Place, in the immediate vicinity of the house and studio he built almost forty years previously, Richard Neutra designed a group of residences in an intimate, harmonious arrangement, where mostly Americans of East Asian origin have settled. The site plan shows this group. Above: View from the west.

The owner of this house and his wife are of East Asian descent, but they, like their own children, were born in California. Like other Japanese people, they provided the most stimulating and satisfying client relationship that an architect could wish, because of their deep unquestioning trust.

These young people had acquired a property that ascended steeply from the street to the east and opened at its upper limit (where there is a double garage) onto an easterly driveway serving as a private road for four properties. From this part of the garage, the building descends stepwise with the slope as far as the front west visitors' entrance, which is reached by means of seven steps leading from the street and then by means of a rock-strewn Japanese garden. On this western front, the master bedroom juts out to form the south section. Like the much more elevated entertaining area on the north side of the west front's expansive lawns, the bedroom overlooks the sea below across a corridor of eucalyptus trees.

Two other homes individually designed by Neutra flank the Ohara home: in the south and somewhat higher is the Akai house, and in the north, somewhat lower is the Flavin house, so that from the even more elevated easterly upper story of the Ohara house (which is mainly the children's bedroom wing) one can look

Above: View from the south. Center: South front of the house. Below: South side of the house gradually ascending the hill.

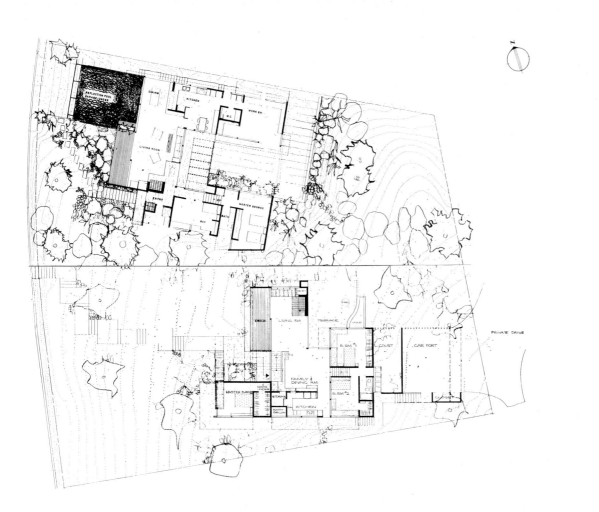

over the Flavin house to the distant northerly mountain chains beyond. This was a significant configurative idea on the part of the designer. Neither in the east courtyard behind the living room fireplace nor on the balcony-terrace facing west and overlooking the three lower-lying Neutra houses below the street (and of course the sea and moun-tain scape beyond) would one recognize the fact that one is actually living in the innermost core of a metropolis of seven million people. Sixty-six-to-seventy-foot lot fronts are happily unified by arrang-ing neighboring plans, providing a satis-fying appearance of spaciousness.

Above: The garage has an entrance from above via an access road meant for several neighbors.

Below: To the east, a spacious patio with view toward the lake in right background.

Above: View through the living room onto the open fireplace and the patio.

Below: View into the living room and onto the balcony-terrace to the west, with the patio to the right.

Above: On clear days, the north window provides an overwhelming view of the mountain panorama illuminated from many sides.

Below: View of the living room, with the west-oriented balcony-terrace to the right.

INADOMI HOUSE, LOS ANGELES, CALIFORNIA

The owners wanted to build their home in the community of Neutra-designed residences overlooking Silver Lake, close to the architect's own home and atelier built almost forty years previously. The site slopes up about one floor level to the southeast and has a grove of young trees across the lake front. The architect was approached at the same time by the owners of the adjacent lot, and the two homes were planned simultaneously in relation to the existing ones he had designed on three sides.

The family includes one girl and three active boys. Both parents work intensively in their business and desired a relaxing atmosphere in which to enjoy their close family life.

The home is oriented in two directions, with all sleeping rooms as well as the living room facing the lake, while the den, family room, and kitchen open to the pool and the hills behind. In addition, the collapsible screen, when open, provides enjoyment to the lake view over the television and music cabinet from the family room and pool. The social rooms were placed at the upper level to be close to the pool and to provide a better view for the living room. Beyond it is the covered connection to the garage, which provides a shaded porch at the shallow end of the pool without supporting posts.

The kitchen, family room, and den are essentially one room used in conjunction with the pool terrace. The den can be chosed off, however, by means of an acoustical accordion door to become a retreat.

The entry door is a half flight down from the living room to allow privacy from the approach. For formal dining, the large, low, architect-designed living room table can be raised by two handles to dining height, and the light upholstered occasional chairs, designed in proportion to the table, are then gathered around it. The sliding door to the master bedroom opens for a more sweeping view across the glass fronts from the bathrooms. A large sliding door opens to the ample deck, which projects to shade the childrens' rooms below.

The children's rooms on the lower level open through their bathroom to the front play yard slightly below and up the outside stairs to the swimming pool. Their hall has a lighted display board along the length of one side. The bedrooms have

Above left: The entrance side of the house.
Below left: The south front.

Above: View from the swimming pool onto the stairwell of the Kambara house; the separating paling fence of redwood now is colorfully overgrown with California grapes. Center: View of the swimming pool. Below: View toward the lake, with swimming pool to the right. As a result of the hill contours, Neutra placed the adjoining buildings of the group on very different levels.

Above: Detail of swimming pool. Center: The back garden with its adjoining rooms for the swimming pool has become an area of constant landscaping and experiments for Japanese gardeners. Visible in the background is Neutra's Flavin house. Below: The kitchen counter with the family breakfast table to the left; in the right background, a view of the lake; to the left, the fireplace masonry, the front of which faces the other side of the living area.

Above right: Ground plan; Inadomi house to the left; and to the right, the Kambara house after it. Below right: Detail view of the living area.

double ceilings to protect against after-bedtime noises from the living room directly above.

The air-conditioning equipment is located in the underfloor space behind the hall and feeds into ducts that run in simple furred spaces on both floors. Built-in indirect lighting is used at important locations for glare-free effect.

The expansiveness to the lovely surroundings, the long low horizontals, and the interiors relate to the overall impression and create the desired positive neural relaxation from wherever one glimpses the house or passes through it.

Dr. Kambara, an American-born Japanese, is a well-known young eye doctor. His property, like the Oharas', is southeast and somewhat higher up on the Silver Lake slope and adjoins the two other Neutra houses, which, together with a fourth, form a truly harmonious, integrated lake front. With Mr. Inadomi, his neighbor to the north, Dr. Kambara shares an imposingly combined, interestingly paved and planted entrance way, which begins at Silver Lake Boulevard near the lake shore, divides under a small pool, and then leads to the two entrance steps of both neighbors. The south steps ascend to the doctor's entrance door which is separated by foliage. Directly upon entering, the visitor faces the door to the right, which leads into the library and the infrequently used home consultation room. The entrant then has in front of him the living room to the south, separated by a curtain. Like the study, it is enhanced by an inviting lake-view balcony. East of this lies a patio and, farther south, the dining

Below left: Ascent from the lake to the entrance of the Kambara house, with the Inadomi house to the left.

Above: Dr. Kambara's house is oriented to the north, without view window, in order not to detract from the privacy of the Inadomis' swimming pool area. Since these early photographs were taken, carefully planted deciduous trees and grape vines have contributed much to separate the neighbors and at the same time have covered the forms of the structure, so that the early pictures provide clear information.

Center and below: The other of the two balconies overlooking the lake.

room, connected to the living room by means of sliding doors. The kitchen, two steps to the east, with its family dining area, is especially useful for this family of many children; one can also serve easily in the garden court and even upstairs, which connects by means of a stairway that is typical of Neutra. The bedrooms there are on the same level as the double garage, which exits to the back onto Argent Place, a street that comes to a dead end to the south and that is the main axis of the Neutra development, near the architect's own house and the Neutra Institute down by the lake.

Above: What looks like walnut paneling is actually a sliding door, which, when opened, frees the view onto the dining table and the stairs that lead left to the private quarters.

Below: Detail of the stairs.

Above: The family takes its meals in the kitchen (left), which is hidden by a wall from the more formal social area but not from the family room in the foreground.

Below: View between the kitchen and stairway through the social area and onto the balcony with its view of the lake, the trees, and the waters of Silverlake, in the center of Los Angeles.

Above: The entrance on the right side; the stairs lead around the masonry of the fireplaces; one of these is located in the sunken family room, which is often doubled in size to become a guest room; the other is on the west side of the living quarters on the upper story. This house, with its view over the Pacific, appears almost Japanese in its lightness of construction.

Below: The massive masonry of the fireplace (unseen to the left) forms a dark contrast to the panorama of the ocean. On very clear days, the Santa Monica Mountains stand out majestically against the outlines of the bay with its surging surf.

KILBURY HOUSE,

Above: Sunsets over the Pacific, clearly seen only on occasion, but often having remarkable cloud formations, are unforgettable in their diversity.

Below: The kitchen participates fully in the significant visual advantages. The north view, expanded by an east window and plate glass, opens to the left onto the transparent front of the living quarters. The sink and drainboard are to the right; the electric stove is directly beneath the northerly ocean-view window.

PALOS VERDES, CALIFORNIA

In Palos Verdes, the natural peninsula overlooking Redondo Bay and the Santa Monica Mountains to the north, the buildable land is often confined to steep slopes and nearly inaccessible hills. A steep curved driveway ends below the living areas, which are located on the upper floor. Only a family room, expanded to make a guest room, is located on the lower story, level with the visitors' parking area. Upon entering the house, one sees the interior stairway ascending at the left, and then the breathtaking view of the bay comes directly into sight, with its coastal towns and the distant rugged mountain chain. From the wide, open front of the living quarters, sliding doors lead to a spacious balcony and, to the east, enlarged by even more glass, into the kitchen, thus affording here, too, an expansive view. The dining area opens on the south to the patio by means of large glass doors with narrow metal frames. In this way, both areas share the panorama. The master bedroom, with its plate glass window high above the stairwell, projects one's view past the living room fireplace to the landscape on the north and enjoys the same view. The remaining bedrooms with their two bathrooms constitute the southerly wing of the house. A steep roof was specified by local regulations, and its interesting treatment of heights determines the main interior rooms.

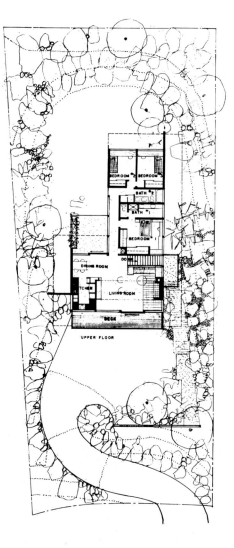

UPPER FLOOR

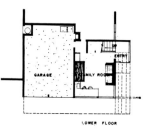

LOWER FLOOR

N

Below: The gable wall, sometimes riotous with color in the sunshine but otherwise dark brown, contrasts with the light wood ceiling under the sloping roof, which was required by the local building authorities. The glass in the background enlarges the view by adding the north part of the kitchen to the visual space of the living room.

Right: To the right of the wall of books is the dining corner, and behind the sliding door is the southeast patio, which serves as an extension of the broad, often windy balcony with its view of the ocean.

FRIEDLAND HOUSE, GLADWYN, PENNSYLVANIA

Above: The visitors' entrance is completely separated from the service entrance, which is used by the children and their numerous friends. Center: View from the southeast chain of hills. Below: East view. Above right: Snowy weather often necessitates the use of the spacious carport. The changing play of shadows enhances the reflections in the pond. Below right: The sleek garden front overlooks the northwest slope of the valley.

The very public-spirited owners have here a progressive milieu for their rich family life and their small art collection, though it is located in a sector of Pennsylvania that retains a conservatism dating back to the eighteenth century. In a distant wooded suburb of Philadelphia, Neutra designed a home with long viewfronts on a wooded property. The entrance road from the east takes the visitor around a reflecting pool under a sharply projecting roof balanced over a glazed entrance front. This is an otherwise windowless masonry wall of washed brick. Upon entering the two-story hall, the visitor glimpses to his right an interesting spiral staircase with cantilevered

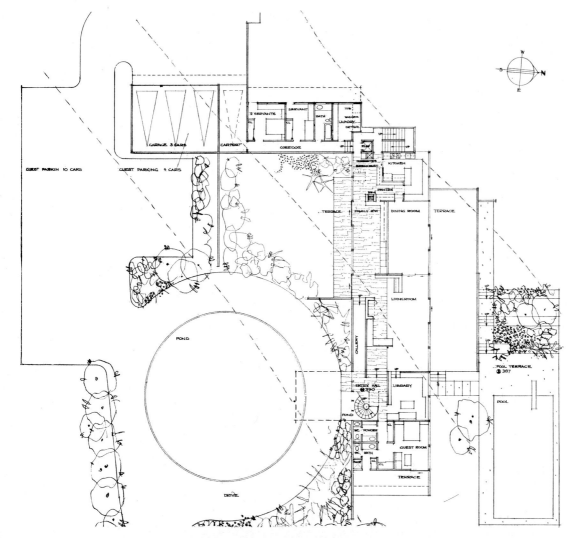

GUEST PARKIN 10 CARS   GUEST PARKING 4 CARS

GARAGE 3 CARS   CARPORT   2 SERVANTS   SERVANT   TUB   BATH   WASHER   LAUNDRY   DRYER   CORRIDOR   UP   KITCHEN   PANTRY

TERRACE   FAMILY RM   DINING ROOM   TERRACE

LIVING ROOM

POND   GALLERY   POOL TERRACE   @ 387

ENTRY HALL   @ 390   LIBRARY   POOL

POND   W.C. POWDER   W.C. BATH   GUEST ROOM   CL

DRIVE   TERRACE   CL

Detail views of the spiral staircase in the entrance hall. Its sculptural form is memorably experienced by the visitor in successive moments.

Above: The open fireplace seen from the east. Center: Through semitransparent curtains, which extend to the right across the long front, one sees into the house with its expansive view over the southern ridge of hills. Below: View from the lower-story children's playroom over the playground and the heated swimming pool, far into the wintry landscape. Right: The kitchen, with its expansive view, becomes an enjoyable work area for the wife. The children's play area is right before her eyes.

treads; this rises above a pool lighted from below, which extends outward through the glass wall. At night, this concealed light source, which originates from a southwesterly niche, casts a fantastic shadow on the easterly massive wall. The visitor's eye is immediately drawn to this as he ascends to the master suite, for instance. Normally the entrance leads him either to the left, and two steps down to the living areas, or straight ahead to the studio at entrance level, or to the background right, where there is a guest suite with bath and an easterly garden terrace.

The living areas extend westward and encompass to the left a bar made of dark wood with built-in and movable seating arrangements by the free-standing fireplace, which is laid up with vertical courses of cut stone, as often utilized by Neutra. The completely glazed north front opens onto a large terrace with steps that lead to the westerly play area one story lower, and to the swimming pool, which also faces west. Beyond this, one looks from above out the window front of the dining room, which is separated from the living room by a mirror wall. Facing southwest is a family room with breakfast nook and plenty of southern exposure to sunlight. Both rooms are connected to a carefully appointed kitchen with built-in cupboards of walnut and stainless steel, an island stove under a vapor hood, and the adjoining utility counters. The service wing facing west is connected by a stairway and an elevator rising to the room-high, glazed sitting area on the upper floor. Here are the children's and master bedrooms with baths and a private terrace for sleeping outdoors and enjoying a sun bath.

MILLER HOUSE,
NORRISTOWN, PENNSYLVANIA

This is the house of a general practitioner devoted to his profession. Set far back from its suburban street, it commands a view past the garden and a swimming pool covered with plastic in winter, toward softly descending meadows that border on the distant woodland. From the entrance, and passing a five-foot-high screen wall, one enters the rear living areas, with their totally glazed fronts. But here there is a protected, cozy sitting corner by the fireplace built of powerful stone masonry, with a similar back wall against a sitting area adjoining the kitchen. Here, too, under the slightly pitched pine ceiling, walnut was used for built-in cupboards, its dark tone contrasting warmly with the bright open view of the landscape and the transparent vestibule of glass, which leads to the swimming pool and the play lawn.

The children's rooms overlook the greenery at the front. At the end of the unobtrusive sleek rambling house is the kitchen. On the garden side, separated from the children's wing and located to the left of the entrance hall, is the parents' suite, with its expansive view.

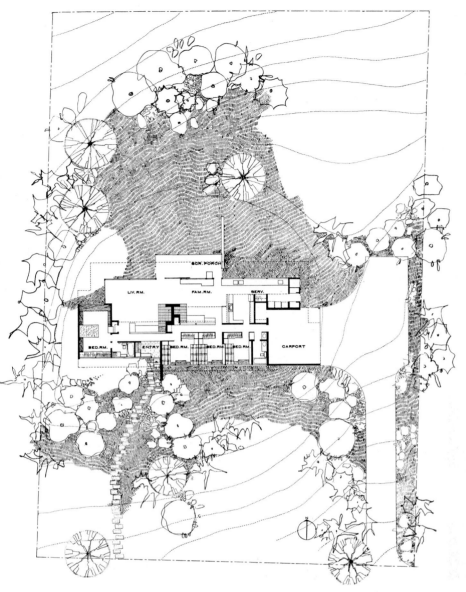

Left: Two views of the swimming pool area. The master bedroom. View from the family room into the living room. Below: By now, the street side of the house is almost completely covered with trees and shrubbery.

Above: The family room and living room are open wide to the landscape. Below: View of the garden outside the living room.

Above: The family room and the adjoining
screened porch. Below: The living room.

HASSERICK HOUSE, PHILADELPHIA, PENNSYLVANIA

Above: The northeast lawn with the master bedroom to the right. Center: View from the northeast onto the garden and patio. Below: The valley front: Right: Patio and lawn.

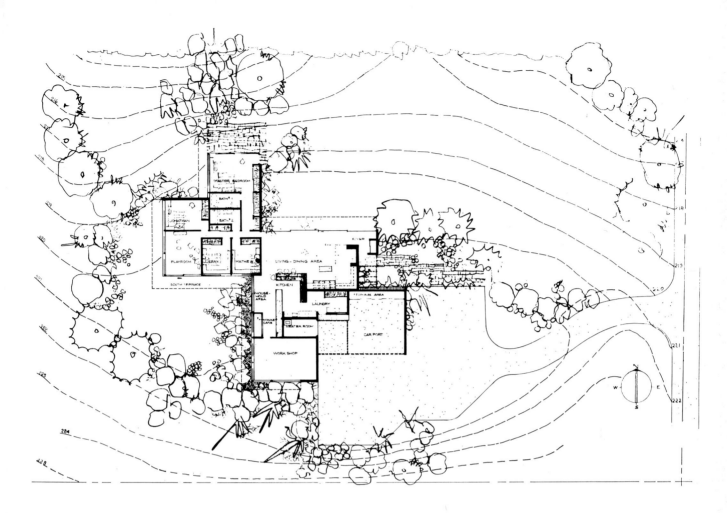

This house was built and later expanded on a lawn extending to charming natural woodland. The entrance hall makes a surprising angle around the fireplace to reach the living area. This has an open garden front, unusually broad even for Neutra, with a massive sliding door. Opposite the door is a pleasantly sheltered sitting corner, serviced by an ingeniously contrived kitchen table below pendent cupboards. From the back of the kitchen one reaches a workshop, while the master and children's bedrooms constitute a wing projection toward the front. The master bedroom, with its one wall closed toward the large paved living-patio, enjoys a view of the sloping and then precipitious garden.

This house is now the residence of Mr. and Mrs. Henry Sawyer.

Above left: The fireplace wall. Below left: The dining area in front of the kitchen counter. Above: The unusually built kitchen counter, with view through the living room and into the garden. Center: The bedroom with its refreshing view of trees. Below: Sitting alcove and serving counter.

COVENEY HOUSE, GULPH MILLS, PENNSYLVANIA

This family is still growing, and an abundance of children was taken into consideration from the very beginning, by choosing a large woodland property that sinks softly southward into a valley, and by having a ground plan expandable to the west. Approach is from the north, along the back stone-faced garage wall, bringing the visitor to a small glassed-in entrance hall. This gives access on the right to the family room and the children's wing; the master bedroom and bath to the left enjoy some measure of seclusion. Directly to the south, the visitor enters the living room with its fireside sitting area to the left. The dining room bay within the southerly, transparent valley-view front, with its sub-stantial roof projection and its wooden terrace along the right, affords a second connection to the den located farther west. The den, like the entire children's wing, enjoys the same southern front as the living room, being only slightly set back. The kitchen, which is illuminated by a skylight, is in the center of the building. Toward the south, the kitchen connects with the dining area; to the west, one looks past a long bar into the den and into the utility room to the north. Thus, the mother and housewife always is in contact with her family, and she can also watch the children while doing her chores, which are considerably lightened by the most modern electrical appliances.

Left: The snow-covered south terrace with the stairway to the garden below. Above: Southwest in summer. Center: Wintry view from the southeast with master bedroom wing to the right. Below right: The south front with view onto a wooded slope. Below left: West view. The sliding doors of the living room and family room open out to the large deck.

After sunset, the continuous exterior lighting eave gives the viewer the feeling that the space continues past the glass front far beyond the south terrace with its plant boxes.

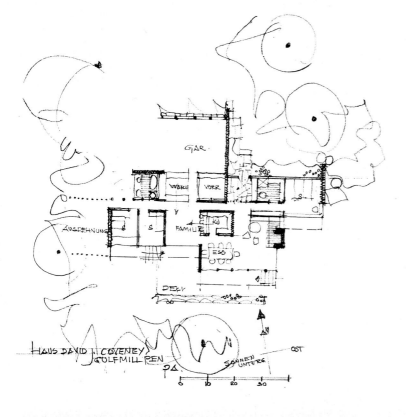

The dining room with pass-through counter and view into the living room.

Above left: The fireplace at the east side of the living room. A mirror placed above the indirect lighting expands space with its visual continuation of the wood ceiling. Above center: Often the children eat at the kitchen counter; to the right, a view into the dining room. Above right: The family room. From both counters, which lighten her housework, the mother can watch the children while attending to her work. A connecting counter is located in the kitchen; the other one is in the laundry room.

Center: The laundry room counter, with left door leading to the children's room, the right one to the entrance door and the master bedroom.

Below: View across the kitchen counter into the playroom, with the laundry room counter to the right.

NINNEMANN HOUSE, CLAREMONT, CALIFORNIA

Above: View from the east; to the right is the bedroom corner with floor-to-ceiling glass, temporarily closed off by an opaque curtain.

Below: View over the pool patio toward the mountains.

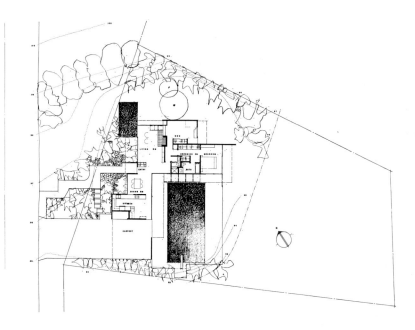

On a promontory above the outskirts of the desert and below a mountain chain is situated the unpretentious house of a young college professor and his wife. It is laid out in an L-shape plan with a swimming pool in the angle of the two wings. From the entrance walk, one can see the carport to the right. The living quarters open at the left to a mountain view, and to the right, via sliding doors, to the swimming pool. The pool is adjacent to the small dining room located beside the very comfortable kitchen, which has its own delivery entrance from the carport. The professor's study at the rear left connects with the living room, which is more oriented to the front by means of a wide trellis composed of slender vertical stainless steel bars; these form the large cage of the family parrot. Here, as on other occasions, Neutra treated a family pet and its quarters as something individualizing, sharing in the determination of the floor plan. The master suite extends eastward toward its own garden exit, with here also a vista over the blue distant mountains beyond the arid desert plains.

Below: View from the south.

Total view of the east front with mountain chain in the north.

The sliding door of the living room at the north end of the "evening side."

The living area opens wide onto the south patio. The parrot has his spacious place of honor and sometimes partakes in people's conversations.

View from the dining room eastward.

The kitchen window toward the west patio.

The driveway.

BARKER HOUSE, PALOS VERDES ESTATES, CALIFORNIA

Above: View northward onto the garden patio with its luxurious plant growth. Below: The entrance path along a wall without windows.
Below right: View from the west toward the entrance, with entrance wall to the right.

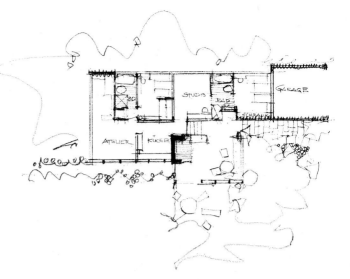

The house is inhabited by two sisters with an artistic bent and visited by like-minded friends. The entrance, approached by a side road and on a level with the garage, is more hinted at than directly seen from the front and the winding hilly street. The living area opens expansively onto the terrace with its panoramic view, high above the often unbelievably blue ocean. With the gable fireplace to the right, a few steps lead up to the dining area and the kitchen beyond. From the south, an elevated studio overlooks the living room, the terrace, and the broad landscape deep below, which stretches to the horizon. The master suite constitutes the east end of the house, while a guest room adjoins the den to the west. A Spanish tile roof was prescribed by the local ordinances of Palos Verdes Estates, and Neutra, as often in such cases, used the gable walls and slanted roof to create large, high interior spaces.

Above: View onto the glazed west gable of the large living room. Below: The large view-window of the living room.

Above: The fireplace area of the living room; to the right, the stairs to the elevated section of the dining area and kitchen.

Below: View from the living room corner toward the coastline.

Left: The elevated study in the background offers a view of the Pacific through the living room.
Above: View from higher level westward.
Below: Bedroom and study.

**OBERHOLTZER HOUSE,
ROLLING HILLS, CALIFORNIA**

The view from the garage toward the entrance way reveals an interesting roof construction.

The entrance way beneath the projecting protective roof.

The master bedroom pleases with its broad transparency but still maintains complete privacy.

From the street, an entry walk zigzags down a remarkable precipice. A driveway descends past the garage side, at the right end of the roof of the house, which was shingled according to local requirements. The entrance adjoins a southerly paved patio, in the outer corner between the garage to the right and the open south front of the living area. A friendly brightness penetrates the house's northern main glass front, and, without being blinded by the sun, one enjoys the view of the distant mountains north of Los Angeles. On this unified open front are also located the master suite at the west end of the floor plan, the open kitchen with its counters east of the social area, and, still farther east, the children's bedrooms.

The sliding glass door connecting the living room to a protected garden patio.

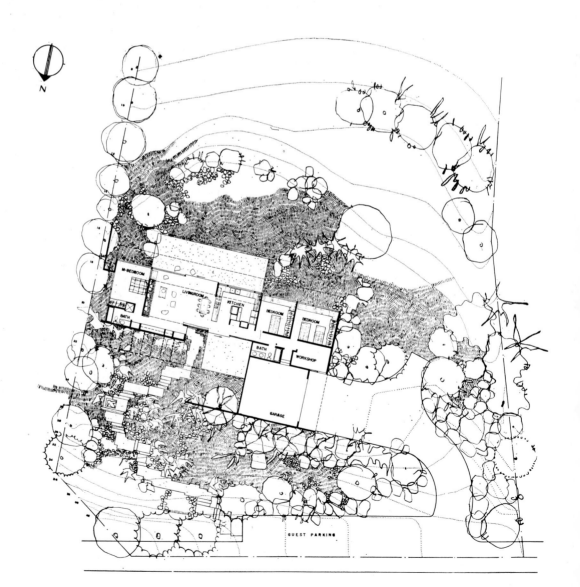

GUEST PARKING

The roof angle that is locally prescribed allowed interesting treatment of ceiling spans in interior rooms. A wall is covered with rough paneling. The built-in furniture and the door are of birch.

The living area also has a broad north glass front and opens eastward into a carefully appointed kitchen.

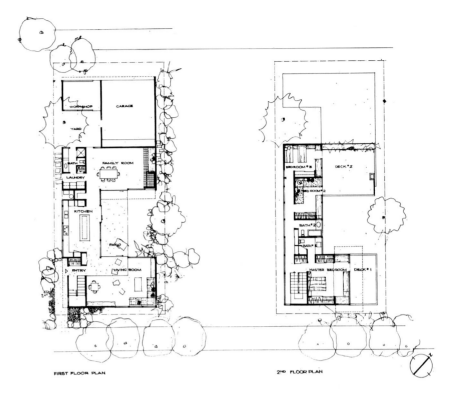

FIRST FLOOR PLAN   2ND FLOOR PLAN

Left: The two-storied north wing, with the bedrooms on the upper story.
Below: The kitchen with dining table.

The den opens to a tree-shaded patio.

View from the kitchen-dining area to the patio corner, with the living room in the background.

Balboa, an island developed and settled as a tourist resort, surrounded by small pleasure boats and boathouses, is the location of this house. Here, on a street with predominantly Spanish colonial-style architecture, is the dwelling of a middle-aged married couple and their two growing daughters. Extremely limited in space, yet with a garage accessible from a back road, the two-story house was required by ordinances to have a shingle roof. The side entrance gives direct access to the main living room as well as to the stairway leading to the upper story. There, the spacious master bedroom and the daughters' rooms look down on the beautiful central patio. Around the patio, everything is grouped, in the shape of a U, with glass fronts: the social room, the kitchen with the family table, and, to the back, the cozy conversation room. Here, the two generations, parents and daughters, can be separated, so that everyone can pursue his own social life undisturbed.

The owners have added a round Danish table and chairs to their living room furniture.

Above: The east front, seen from the swimming pool. Below: The easterly trellis front frames the often misty but sometimes clear mountain view.

CLARK HOUSE, PASADENA, CALIFORNIA

The owner, a music pedagogue, and his wife and daughters are sensitively aware of the landscape around the family home, which is reached by winding streets and enjoys from its vantage point the eternal dynamism of the mountain weather north and east of Pasadena Valley.

The children's wing is to the left of the service entrance and carport, which is directly connected with the kitchen and its refreshing view over the greenery. From the kitchen one can serve a westerly garden court as well as the easterly dining room, which adjoins the living room and has the same view over the swimming pool. The master bedroom is secluded at the south end of the house.

Above: The southeast corner of the house and view into the westerly landscape. Center: Detail of entrance. Below: View from the terraced slope down to the driveway.

119

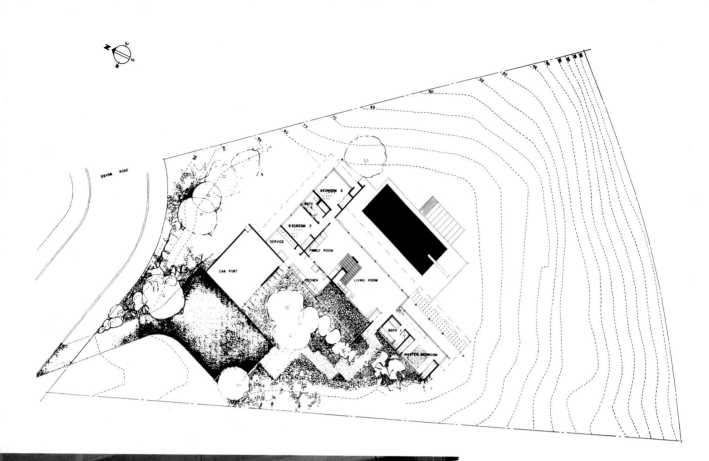

View of the northern Sierra mountain chain, now mist-covered but often suddenly emerging unbelievably clear over the valley fog, to be reflected in the pool.

Above: View from the family room toward the living room and terrace. Below left: View into the southerly bedroom wing. Below right: The kitchen overlooking the outdoors; the living room, with its view northward to the family room.

BOND HOUSE, SAN DIEGO, CALIFORNIA*

For an architect like Neutra, an unoccupied house, devoid of greenery and planting, is only an abstract beginning. One can only try to anticipate the future interlocking development of the family that will live there. The inorganic form of rigid, static constructions is only the foundation for what the architect is planning. He foresees future life-dynamics through which vitality will be bestowed upon what is built. A transparent front will connect the interior with the exterior living terrace. Now all is still gray and barren, unadorned with human comforts such as chaises longues and other furniture, still uninhabited by those who hope to feel at home here for decades with their friends and guests. The architect must try to anticipate, to live in his imagination in the unseen future.

The exposed tooled joints of the masonry foundation wall that supports the terrace will soon be refreshingly concealed with climbing plants and reflected in the water of the swimming pool, like the blue of the far-flung sky and the white of the billowing clouds. A trellis will no longer seem like an empty framework but will be overgrown with masses of foliage and decorated with blooming vines. A children's swing, without laughing children, and the distant, silent country, without enlivening foreground planting, are here only an architect's promise, which must still be kept.

First come the many drawings and plans, which are communicated to the man who seeks counsel for his future and who trusts the architect if they are explained in friendly dialogues. Then, week by week, the technical building process takes place. And finally, life moves in, making the still-naked shell into something ever-more close to nature on the exterior, and enlivening and invigorating the interior through years of habitation.

In the midst of an industry-standardized, ordinance-prescribed, monotonously normalized world of appearances, each individual dwelling is a prototype. It can serve as an example to show that the personalized is redeeming and to encourage a focus on "biological individuality" — an idea that scientists value highly. Even in his large-scale developments, Neutra always tried to learn from the individual case. Even in a beautiful, expansive countryside — and not only

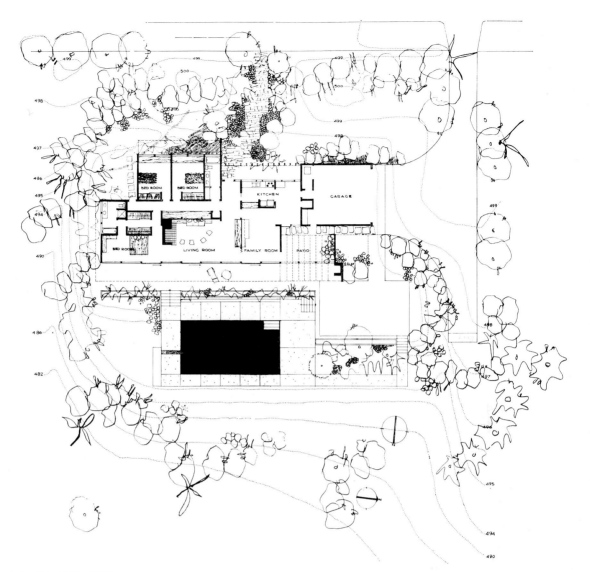

A broad glass front to the north offers a splendid view. The wide stairway connects the living terrace with the level of a planned reflecting and swimming pool, the focal point of future hospitality.

in dense, metropolitan areas — one can sadly lack nearness to nature. The most precious materials, the greatest geometric spaciousness do not deepen and enrich our lives as does subtle "nature-nearness," closeness to the organic, which, after all, formed primeval man and equipped him with the senses and nerves for his future development. All architecture — everything in this book — Neutra always understood as something to be gardened and "greened over." Even in restricted space, he aimed to build in nature.

* This house is now the residence of the Koots family.

OYLER HOUSE, LONE PINE, CALIFORNIA

The unpretentious low-set home of this large family is situated on a craggy plateau above Lone Pine, California, 300 miles east of Los Angeles. The name of the place corresponds well to the solitary house in its rocky surroundings. A serpentine street winds among craggy mountains whose form and color seem to change with the sun's position, making the approach a dramatic event. Two mighty boulders jut out at the northeast corner of the large, arid piece of land. The masonry on the west and north is made of stone that the owner, a member of the Mormon faith, collected on the property. Other building material had to be hauled long distances to the site. Upon entering the house, one sees that dividing the hall from the living area and near to the fireplace is a low bookcase. Farther to the south are the den, with its informal atmosphere and the almost square kitchen with its dining table (with storage space below) and built-in island stove. This modest dining area is extraordinarily enhanced by the westerly pan-

Above left: View from the west. The shadow of another rock plays on the rough surface of one of the huge, stacked-up boulders. With the exception of the stone wall, there is a definite contrast between the clean-cut geometrical lines of the house and the background of nature, which is thus better honored by contrast than by assimilated form. Below left: Unhewn boulders and rocks become part of the masonry. Inyo County and Mount Whitney, drawings by Richard Neutra. Above: The wild jagged silhouette of snowbound nature above man's simple geometry. The highest mountain chain in the contiguous continental United States runs parallel to the modest, low roof of the Mormon family home. Center and below: The swimming pool was dynamited out of a cliff.

orama over the snowcapped mountain chain, which is crowned by Mount Whitney.

The children's quarters and a play area are oriented to the south. In the north wing is the parents' bedroom (which they graciously loaned to their architect at Christmas). In winter, the adjacent dressing room and bath have an unsurpassable view of the icy cliffs and snowy wilderness. The mitered glass corner of the master bedroom and its broad opening to the east allow surveyal of the whole countryside. In its midst are the colossal twin rocks, whose light and shadow plays change fascinatingly from dawn to dusk and are dramatic even by

Above and left: Glass is not only wonderful for the view onto a breathtaking landscape. When one stands before the house, one sees the reflection of the giant cliffs in the view windows directly opposite the beds of the nature-loving Mormon couple. Center left: View to the northeast. The shadows on the mountain chain change minute by minute. Below left: Transparency and reflection beneath a wood ceiling, which projects as an eave over the windows across the entire length. Below right: View down toward the lake, which up to 1910 offered the eye a water surface sparkling in the sun; now there remains only the gleam of a white layer of salt.

moonlight. A large swimming pool, dynamited into a giant flat-topped boulder, is reached by climbing a few chiseled steps.

For the Mormon family living there, this is no "solitary house." Both parents and children feel that it is embedded deeply in the universal landscape.

Above left: From the mitered glass corner of the master bedroom, one enjoys a northward view that is never monotonous and often is fantastically illuminated. Below left: Mount Whitney in spring snow.

Since future residences on the other side of the access road may one day impede this view, the architect decided upon high windows facing only this mountain chain and opened the main front of the house eastward onto the client's own rocky land. Above: Bathroom windows, which actually should refresh, are usually high, small, and inadequate; but when a house stands alone in a mountain landscape, without a privacy problem, it is uplifting to enjoy the quickly changing mood of the landscape reflected in a large mirror, while brushing one's teeth. Below: Because this big family of modest means could not afford a separate dining room, a large table, with built-in burners and cupboards below, must accommodate the whole family in the kitchen. The captivating vista onto the Mount Whitney chain compensates for the somewhat restricted space.

MASLON HOUSE, CATHEDRAL CITY, CALIFORNIA

Above? The access road, with snow-covered Mount Jacinto towering up from the misty background above the oasis. Below: A trellised pathway leads into the wind-protected inner court and to the main entrance.

Facing page, above left: Scorching desert sun over the cooling pool. Above right: A curved slatted fence throws its shadow and visually screens the swimming pool from the visitors' entrance in the garden. The house is magnificently located at the edge of the golf course oasis, with high mountain silhouettes in the distance. Center. The house in its closest relation to the sparkling blue swimming pool. To the left is "The Guardians," a three-figure sculpture by Kenneth Armitage. Below: Olive trees, shaped in the Japanese tradition, form the almost changeless foreground accent for the house, behind the three Guardians.

For more than a generation, Richard Neutra was creatively stimulated by the problem of desert habitation in the individual case or within an extensive development, as in Arizona. For all its anthropological past and its designation in many a language as "the devil's playground," the desert with its oases is expandable by technology. It can become the catch-basin of the earth's growing population, as Neutra saw in his studies of northwestern Pakistan and Africa as well as in America. Experimental building here, in this climate

Above: A large roof overhang and terrace protect the glass front of the living room. In the foreground is a sculpture by Lipschitz. Below: The large terrace in front of the living quarters seems to go directly over into the green of the oasis.

which in many respects is still untried, will reveal many of the problems and technical details connected with the socially significant building activity of tomorrow.

A couple with a large circle of family

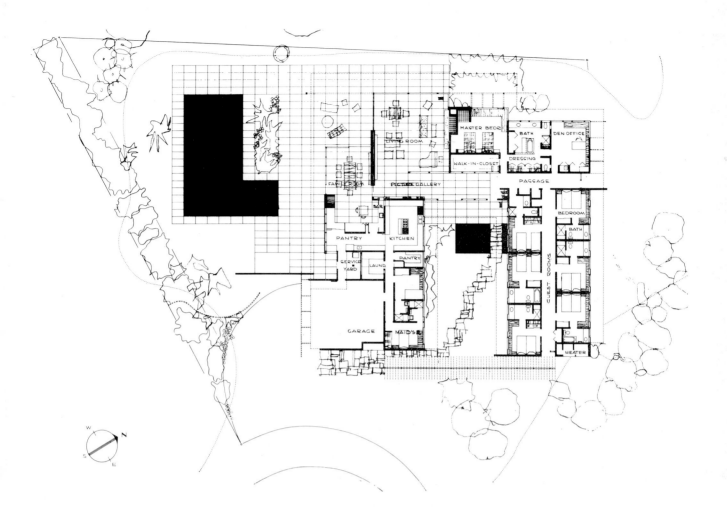

Detail of the master bedroom, with a miter-joined glass window and a view into the green oasis.

Above: View from the terrace into a corner of the living room. To the right of the fireplace is a metal sculpture by Arp. Center: View from the living room into the dining room, with the pass-through counter to the kitchen on the right. The sliding doors hide a technically elaborate steam table. To the left is the bar with its necessary equipment. The mirror over the sliding doors creates depth in the room and continues the illuminated ceiling. Below: Grill and dining alcove by the sideboard, with family room to the right.

and friends and with an extraordinary interest in art lives in this building and has enriched it over the years with its collection of art treasures.

An almost mysteriously hidden entrance leads to the passageways and to an inner courtyard, which is protected from the desert winds. To reach the main entrance, one crosses over a reflecting pool. The children's and guest rooms are to the right of the hall. In the north part are the bedroom and study of the indefatigable master of the house. Facing the west and the swimming pool are the living room and its partly covered terrace, and the family room, which adjoins the dining room with its grill and bar. The kitchen and service wings evolve southward from the garden court.

Above: The owner's study with built-in desk, couch, and telephones that connect him with his law practice thousands of miles away in Minneapolis, Minnesota. Center: View over the dining table westward, with grill to the left. Below left: View from the master bedroom, with dresser to the right. Below right: Window and mirror over the built-in sink offer a refreshing view into the oasis landscape.

Above: View from the dining room over the swimming pool and toward the dimly seen mountain chain; to the left, the sculpture "The Guardians." Right: The north side of the living room, view along the bedroom wing. Beneath the trellis to the right is the sculpture "Singing Man" by Barlach.

RICE HOUSE, LOCK ISLAND, RICHMOND, VIRGINIA

Above: The house is carefully fitted to the extremely difficult, dramatic cliff site. Below: The water-surrounded terrace, the swimming pool beneath, and the current of water beyond lend dynamic interest to the landscape. Above right: Huge boulders form a primeval setting for the geometricity of man-made architecture. Below right: The round-disc stairs lead from the balcony-terrace, which is surrounded by shallow water and has no landing, down to the swimming pool built directly into the cliffs. In the dark background, deep below, the water of the St. James River, from which the rocky island that bears this house projects about 135 feet.

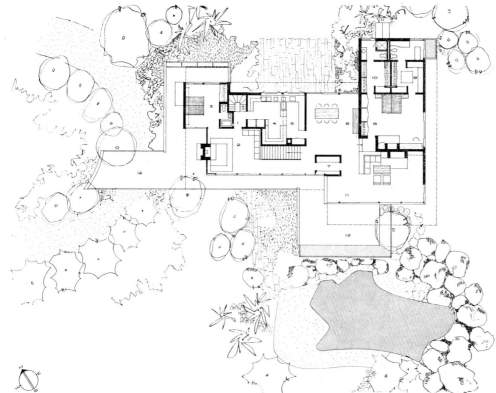

1 Upper entrance
2 Japanese room
3 Guest room
4 Kitchen
5 Service
6 Dining room
7 Bar
8 Master bedroom
9 Dressing room
10 Dressing room
11 Living room
12 Terrace

Above left: The water surface of the river with its rushing currents can be seen in the background; above it, the swimming pool, which has been freely dynamited out of the rocky slope.

Above: Sculptural, mushroomlike forms serve as steps from the bathing terrace and island boulders to the upper balcony. Below: A broad, carpeted stairway and glazed walls expand the view onto the landscape.

Above and center left: In the background, the wooded river valley on the other side of the water protectively surrounds the balcony-terrace. Center right: The guests leave their cars here to enter the house from the left. Below: The garage driveway from the back of the house, with plentiful turning space. Facing page: View upward over the swimming pool.

A craggy island projects 135 feet above water-level and has a view of the St. James River, with its rapids and silent upstream waters. Layouts and detailed perspective sketches were redrawn half a dozen times, so as to fit the house carefully to the extremely difficult yet fascinating site. Strategically placed trees about the hilltop were spared. The access road was oriented from north to east and connected with the bridge on the riverbank which was then under construction. The main entrance was sheltered by a wind-blocking wall, which supports a projecting entrance roof. Visitors immediately have a stupendous view over the river terrace to the southwest, down the slopes, and onto the water flowing by.

From the entrance hall, a straight stairway leads upward. Below, to the right, is the access to two guest rooms.

The main stairs lead up to a large room, which can be separated by curtains and sliding doors to make a dining room to the east and a social area to the southwest. The family room extends to the west and north, where, from comfortable chairs on each side of the fireplace, one can see past a north-oriented terrace to the landscape beyond. The living room has its own balcony-terrace facing west, and opposite it, on the east wall, a large fireplace with a sitting area. From here, one can look in various directions toward open country. Even the dining room extends into the landscape onto another terrace, this one facing east, from which stairs lead into the garden.

The master suite is raised a few steps and thus has en even more private atmosphere. From its west window can be seen the social area below and beyond. When the curtains are drawn back, one can, from a higher vantage point, again have a gratifying view over the river. The bedroom's transparent sliding doors open onto a southerly terrace, the view from which, like that facing west, is unrestricted by railings. Instead, a strip of water (heated in winter), within a shallow, dark, anodized aluminum container, prevents stepping forward to the edge of the terrace, and permits a much closer contact with the landscape. Clouds and treetops are reflected vividly in the water.

GLEN HOUSE, STAMFORD, CONNECTICUT

This house lies in a beautiful, somewhat thinned-out forest. Large boulders and a magnificent vista of wooded hills to the south enrich the site with the visual variety created by seasonal changes.

The family for whom this modest home was designed consisted of three small children and their parents. The father commuted to New York and, since he was often away on business trips, he wanted his living room to accommodate his get-togethers with his family and guests during his precious hours at home. The den was also used as the parents' sitting area or study, when they wanted to be by themselves. These two rooms, as well as the vestibule and the master bedroom, nestle between two groups of trees and rock, and are expanded southward by a view into a clearing, making the rooms especially enjoyable for their winter sun. The kitchen and the other bedrooms face east to the children's playground. A maximum of seclusion is provided by the access road from the northwest to the entrance and into the inner corner of the L-shaped house. A carport and a fourth bedroom (also used as a guest room) are on a somewhat lower level at the north end of the house.

The use of cedar, Philippine mahog-

any, and sensitively harmonizing paints contributes to the desired effect of simple, modest coziness. Openness to the dynamic coloration of the charming surroundings demands and everywhere assures their dominance, but one can hardly reproduce this fully in black-and-white photography.

This house is now the residence of Victor Bisherat.

Below left: The southwest corner, where the master bedroom is located, is somewhat separated from the children's and guest room wing to the northeast. In the right background, the southerly glazed elevation, seen here from the inside, with its low vents. Above: View from the southerly valley. The sunniest corner of the master bedroom is shaded especially to the west and south. The south front of the living room and master bedroom is fully transparent; the low aluminum vents are inserted into this glass front for carefully studied, microclimatic reasons, and open almost directly onto the lawn by the forest clearing. Center: The westerly entrance court amid tall stands of timber, with carport to the left and stairway to the centrally located entrance hall, from which one reaches the southerly living room wing and the family bedroom wing at the northeast. Below: View of the winter-heated water roof, of whose existence one is only dimly aware but which reflects the densely wooded landscape from various sides, so that it resembles a pond in a forest clearing.

Above left: The children's play area in the vicinity of the kitchen entrance, acoustically separated from the entertainment veranda by a massive wall. Above: The kitchen bay of the utility room. The daylight streaming in through the east window is complemented by a skylight above the built-in stove. Below: Westward view across the living room along the southerly valley-view front onto the sleek fireplace and the distant west window of the master bedroom. The separating wall to the right is not full-height, so that the living room ceiling extends pleasingly over the entrance hall.

LIST HOUSE, GRAND RAPIDS, MICHIGAN

This house, the residence of a well-known brain surgeon and his wife, is also blessed with a magnificent view. From the master bedroom windows in the left wing, and especially from the living room to the right by the garden balcony, one looks over the sparse woods and across to a small lake.

The ascent from the driveway to the entrance winds past carefully preserved trees to a little entrance bridge, which skillfully brings the visitor into the center of the circulation plan. From the front, one looks through the living room and across the lake; to the left, near the kitchen, the stairs lead downward to the garage and the utility rooms. To the right of the entrance hall and eastward up the slope are two guest bedrooms which await the welcome visit of children and grandchildren.

The owner, a devoted doctor active in research, has only the evening hours to recover from his long day's work. The night-time illumination of his house is of special importance to him and has thus in this case been impressively made visible to the reader.

Below: The simple wood skeleton of the house and its beamed ceiling stand out especially clearly in the evening light. The garden court to the left is now luxuriously overgrown with flowering shrubs where the balcony stairs reach the terrain. Right: The illuminated entrance stairway.

View from the fireplace bench toward the lake vista, which delightfully enhances this room on moonlit evenings with its reflections in the water.

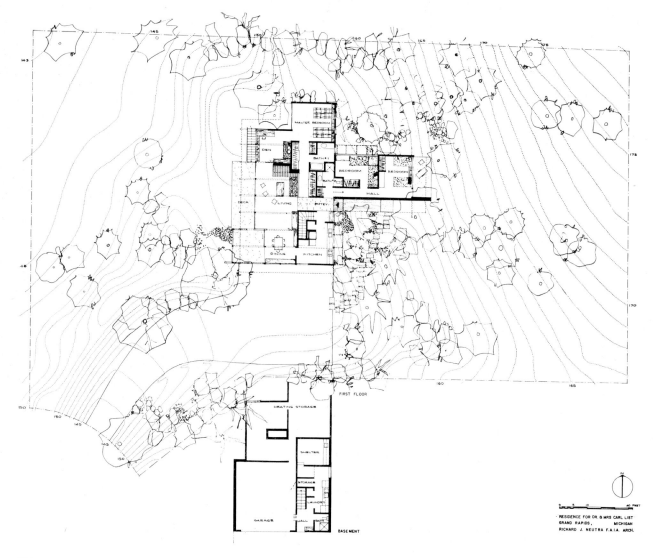

RESIDENCE FOR DR. & MRS CARL LIST
GRAND RAPIDS, MICHIGAN
RICHARD J. NEUTRA F.A.I.A. ARCH.

Above: View over the dining table into the living room. Below: The living room and the library to the left, seen from the lake-view balcony; the dining room is to the right, but out of view in this picture.

KEMPER HOUSE, WUPPERTAL, GERMANY

Above: View from southwest into the westerly living room trellis; to the left, the bath house with swimming pool and sauna. Below: General view from the south; both stories of the house overlook the south slope. Above right: The rambling east-west oriented house is restfully settled into the landscape. Below right: Closeup view from the east, with the long, six-foot-high garden wall, which separates the entrance court in the right background from the garden to the south.

Like some other Neutra homes, this one also enjoys a southern exposure and a sunny slope and has a tall stand of timber. The layout shows the access road from the north, from which the visitor immediately enjoys an expansive view under the upper floor and into the southerly landscape, before he proceeds to the entrance hall to the right. From here, one can enter the studio to the left and the spacious living room to the west, which is raised three steps, or go up the stairs to the right of the entrance to reach the bedroom story. This upper story is essentially L-shaped, with powder room, bath, and master bedroom having their own covered terrace above the east garage, all commanding a magnificent view to the south. To the right of the landing stretches the row of children's bedrooms, with west windows and a balcony-terrace.

Below, on the main floor, the west front of the dining room faces a patio,

A Ground floor
1 Entrance
2 Workroom
3 Living room
4 Dining room
5 Maid's room
6 Drying room
7 Utility hall
8 Utility room
9 Cold-storage room
10 Kitchen

B Upper floor
1 Child's room
2 Patio
3 Reflecting pool
4 Guest room
5 Closet
6 Shower
7 Bath
8 Hallway
9 Toilet and washroom
10 Hallway
11 Women's room
12 Dressing room
13 Master bedroom
14 Terrace

C Bath house
1 Reflecting pool
2 Swimming pool
3 Wading pool
4 Sump pump
5 Anteroom
6 Sauna

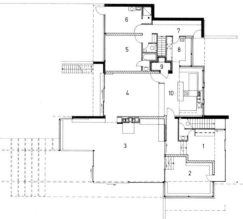

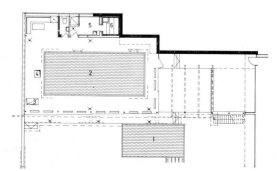

Above left: General view from the south-east, with the tree-covered hills in the background. Above: View from above, from the east. Center: View onto the covered entrance, with a water roof, above left, in front of the eastern terrace. Below: The carport.

which affords a view over reflecting water toward the swimming pool. The patio also has a waterroof that mirrors the tree-tops. After sunset, when the patio and the towering tree trunks are illuminated with a color like the mild white of the moon, the evening view offers a gentle tranquillity. Even at night, all rooms extend into the garden landscape.

Above: View from the north. Below: The open entrance hall with access between the reflecting pools. Above right: View from the library of the study through the somewhat elevated living room and westward. Below right: The fireplace, seen from the sitting alcove at the northeast end of the living room.

Closeup view from the west into the living room toward the fireplace and the northeast corner of the living room. To the right, the south terrace with the sunken study in the background.

Above: Westward view through the living room into the evening landscape. Below: The sitting alcove of the living room.

RANG HOUSE, KÖNIGSTEIN, GERMANY

Above: Clouds above the August landscape. Right: The entrance steps.

The residence for this well-known pedagogue at the Johann Wolfgang Goethe
University was built on a large wooded
plateau of the Taunus, not far from
Frankfurt. Access is from the south, with
a view toward the living side of the
house and the forest beyond. The driveway to the cellar garage and the main
entrance are on the west side. A few
steps lead to the lobby; then one passes
the central hall and enters the living
room with its sunken square sitting
area beside an open fireplace. This
separates the owner's rear study, from
which one can directly reach the master
bedroom and the bath. Both the living
room and the study open to the south.
The remaining rooms evolve from the
central hall with its covered outdoor sitting and play area facing east. The

dining room, the outdoor covered dining
area, and the water surface of the flat
garage roof are perpendicular to the
kitchen with its back entrance and stairs
leading to the cellar. A connecting corridor evolves into the children's sleeping
quarters to the north. These rooms open
eastward, with a view onto a pool, or
westward toward the valley and the
Schloss Königstein.

The exterior layout of this beautiful
home corresponds to its clear spatial arrangement. Laid out in a T-shaped
formation, the living, dining, and utility
areas, as well as the children's sleeping
quarters, adjoin the hall with its raised
ceiling. The three reflecting pools take
up the main axes of the building and
lead to the garden areas with their broad
lawns and sparse but effective planting.

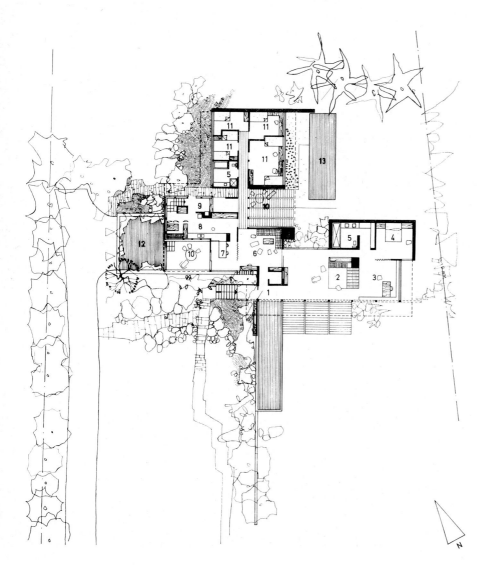

1 Entrance
2 Living room with sunken fireplace sitting area
3 Study
4 Master bedroom
5 Bathroom
6 Central living room
7 Dining room
8 Kitchen
9 Entrance from garage and storage rooms on lower floor
10 Terrace with sitting area
11 Children's bedroom
12 Water surface on the garage roof
13 Garden patio with pool

Left: The entrance from the west. Above: The lighting at night. Below: Periwinkle and evergreens along the quarrystone wall extending into the garden.

Extreme left: Children's playpool. Left: View from the north onto the front reflecting pool. Below: Only a few steps to the right, and the mirror-smooth surface of the pool comes into view.

Above: The garage and utility entrance side of the house. Below: The living room north front with its reflection of the landscape that overlaps with the direct view to the other side.

Above: A wintry evening, easterly view. Center: The stone fireplace with cushioned sunken seating area is centrally located. Below left: View from the work desk into the living room. Below right: The circular skylight allows the noonday sun to enliven the floor and the interior space, which is located far away from the glass fronts protected by roof overhangs.

Above: The library, seen southward. Center: View eastward. Below left: Even on a cloudy day, one's vision is enhanced here. Going from the living area into the vestibule to the right, one feels the contrast between the rough stone masonry and the mirroring glass. Below left: Each sunray brings changes of light into the interior, as happens with the vertical wood slats by the entrance.

Facing page, above left: A skylight interestingly illuminates the covered easterly garden terrace. Above right: Two eastward views of the entrance hall, by day and by night. Below: The easterly and southerly garden can be seen from the upholstered sitting area of the entrance hall.

Above: View from living room northward and reflection of its southerly glass front. Below: From the sunken fireplace sitting area, one can see past the southerly and northerly glazed fronts.

CASA TUJA,
ASCONA, SWITZERLAND

Above: A driveway winds up from the valley and makes a turn toward the south-oriented garden entrance. Below: View into the subtropical lake valley. Above right: A two-story residence on a steeply rising property. Large wooded parks surround the land on three sides. The glass front affords a panoramic view onto Lago Maggiore deep down in the valley.

On a sloping site and practically surrounded by towering trees, this house overlooks Lago Maggiore, the medieval city of Ascona, and the mountain chains to the north, east, and south. Unless they motor up the curved drive to the south end of the house, visitors can approach on foot from a lower parking area by ascending to the main front entrance past the open, projecting terrace, to a garden stair at left and a reflecting pool at right, which also, through the plate glass, extends into the indirectly illuminated entrance hall. An entrance powder room and bathroom to the right also serve two agreeably spacious guest rooms, with their own garden areas accessible through sliding glass doors. The western corrdor with its effectively concealed lighting doubles as a gallery for changing art displays.

The main story, with a magnificently wide view northeast and southeast over the lake, has a slightly elevated westerly portion oriented to the kitchen and servants' area. This leads to a paved patio under tall trees, on the westerly rise

behind the house. The southwesterly dining area is related to the tree-adorned garden court in its rear. From the dining room — which opens broadly into the spacious living quarters and onto its balcony-terraces south and east — the major parts of the house, most of its vistas, and all the changing dynamics of the magnificent landscape are enjoyed.

In the living quarters, which also command the same views, a well-articulated, neatly upholstered sitting corner is diagonally opposite the tall fireplace wall which continues vertically the light, slightly variegated marble flooring. The narrow-profiled, darkly stained coniferous wood of the high ceiling contrasts with the blond hardwood of the sitting corner, low bookshelves, and the partition joining and backing it. This partition affords privacy to the wide stairway, which leads up from the main visitors' entrance in the lower story.

The low, broad fireplace opening can be closed with a horizontally sliding aluminium panel. Adjacent to the fireplace wall is a tall, collapsible door that

closes toward the large glass fronts on the east, next to the lake-vista terrace. When this folding door is collapsed, the glass front continues into the study with its spacious desk. High bookshelves are behind the comfortable desk chair, which faces the panoramic view; and on the south another fireplace backs that of the living room.

Next to the study, in the northeast corner, is the master suite, with its articulated dressing room and bath. This is also accessible directly from the upper stair leading through an interesting by-pass corridor, which opens broadly to a square, spacious, trellised, planter-surrounded end terrace that looks out on a neighboring wooded estate. (Wherever feasible, Neutra tried to "borrow" landscape enjoyment from space beyond legal boundary lines and used planting to screen off visual features that were competitive, disturbing, or undesirable.) Extensive mirroring over the double lavatory counter gives a spacious appearance to the master bathroom, while

the sunken tub appears to be almost outdoors when the drapes are drawn open from the floor-to-ceiling plate glass. Italian mosaic tile, with contrasting dark and light hues, other kinds of wall surfaces, and indirect or translucent illumination play a more important role than do lighting fixtures as such.

The lower story, directly accessible from the garage, contains ample utility areas and elaborate installations for climate control.

This house is, in principle, a steel construction, framed over the reinforced concrete base structure of the ground floor. Contrasting materials — the anodized aluminum for sliding doors, glass, light and dark hardwood, polished marble, and more roughly surfaced stone pavement — harmonize with the constantly changing natural environment on the outside of the house.

Nighttime illumination, dark background silhouettes, and shadows dramatize the residence and its surroundings. (Now, further enhanced by gardening, the house is even more incorporated into the landscape.)

Above: Visitors enjoy the main facade and enter between a free-standing exterior stairway, on the left, and, on the right, a reflecting pool which, with its planting, continues into the interior. Below: The terrazzo steps of the broad main stairway, rising between beautiful grained wood wainscoting, are ascended by visitors when they come from the central entrance or driveway to go up to the living room.

Above: View into the living room. Below: Sketch of the living room, the elevated dining room level at the left, with its garden- and forest-oriented patio in the background.

Above: The living room connects openly in its northwest corner with the dining room placed several steps higher. Center: Design sketch of the interior from the south. Below: Looking through the dining room southward, one overlooks the living area, the balcony-terrace, and the expansive landscape.

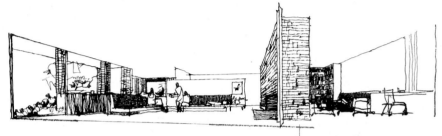

A Ground floor

1 Living room
2 Study
3 Sun deck
4 Master bedroom
5 Terrace
6 Roman bath
7 Bath
8 Dressing room
9 Closet
10 Maid's room
11 Guest toilet
12 Ironing room
13 Kitchen
14 Dining room
15 Patio
16 Utility courtyard
17 Garage entrance
18 Woodside garden

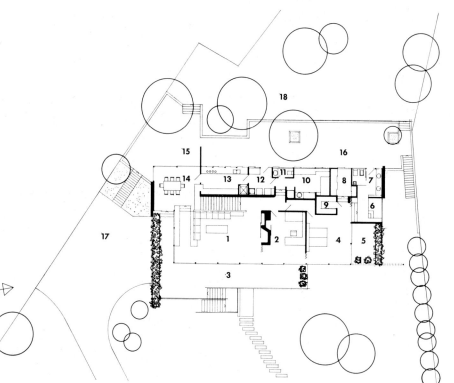

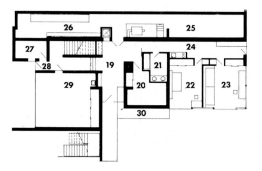

B Garden floor

19 Entrance hall
20 Storage space
21 Guests' bath
22 Guest room
23 Guest room
24 Gallery
25 Cellar
26 Equipment room
27 Wine cellar
28 Service entrance
29 Double garage
30 Decorative pool

Above left: The owner's study, seen from the broad window front. Below: View from the owner's work desk.

Above left: The bedroom corner to the southeast opens wide into the landscape. Below left: Even the master bedroom shares in the transparent south front and in the view down into the lake valley.

Above: The sunken bath with its floor of small tiles. Below: Glass mosaic walls reach up to the dark, finely profiled pine ceiling. Total transparency toward the landscape brings this bathroom close to nature and makes bathing much more invigorating.

HOUSE IN THE SWISS ALPS, NEAR WENGER, SWITZERLAND

This house, with its powerful panorama of the Alps culminating in the snowfield of the Jungfrau, has a view as can seldom be enjoyed by man. The driveway from the mountain railway station approaches from the north, and the visitor reaches the house from above, in the direction of the magnificent view. He is received in the screened-off vestibule, which is separated from the living room by a wall that does not quite reach the ceiling. To the left are a washroom, a clothes closet, while to the right is a stairway to the lower story. On the west side, an elevator connects the kitchen beyond with the rooms and storage areas of the lower story. All the important rooms have broad high windows oriented toward the southern landscape, and the part of the upper story that opens onto a terrace from the south wall has a somewhat higher ceiling. The fire-

place of the social area, located where the lower ceiling is elevated, is placed so that from its spacious but cozy conversation alcove one can overlook the fire, the terrace, the valley, and the mountains beyond.

Sliding doors extend this living room to the terrace, and an optional visual separation in the form of folding doors or curtains permits expansion westward into the dining room (which is serviced directly from the kitchen to the north). The living room can expand eastward as well, by opening to the library, which connects with the master bedroom in the southeast corner. This room is also accessible from the entrance hall by way of the dressing room. One can also reach the owner's studio from there. Since the owner gets up early in order to follow the morning illumination with the eye of an artist, the east-oriented

Above left: The moon has risen in the mist high in the firmament. This and succeedings photographs render only incompletely the dynamic natural scene, to which Neutra tried to relate his use of shape and form. Center left: The contrast is sharp and clear. Below left: High cirrus clouds in the early morning, when the Jungfrau still stands in its own shadow and the valley is enveloped by mist.

Above: Toward noon. Cumulus clouds float slowly over mountains and glacier crevices, which glisten in the sunlight. Below: Valley view from the mountain slope, from which one descends to the house.

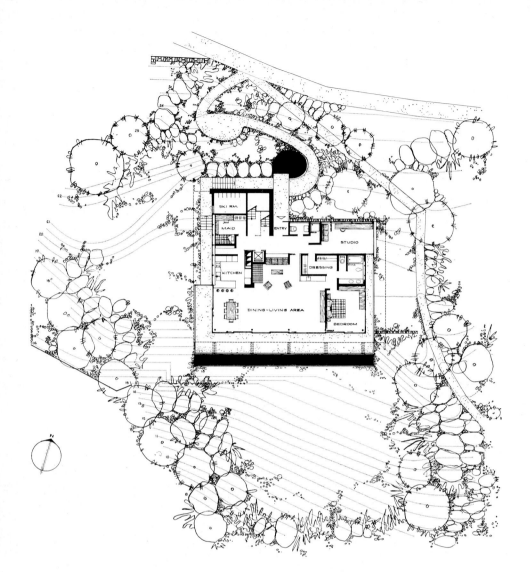

Center: One of the first designs with a flat water roof, which in summer reflects the heat rays and in winter is heated so that the snow melts. The view front, with its partly adjustable sun-shielding devices, faces the most spectacular scene (consisting of glaciers, clouds, and atmospheric dynamism) before which Neutra ever had the privilege of building. Right: The integration of the habitat with the surrounding growth was as important to Neutra as the relationship of the interior rooms to the mighty view; he shielded them climatically, but opened them visually to the eternal play of the universe.

Above left: Dawn. Neutra thought it would be more harmonious to echo certain gentle diagonals of the mountain outlines in the roof profile than to use an arbitrary dramatic gable steepness. Below left: The eastern front. In order not to impede the view from the living room into the valley, the wall by the balcony railing on the south side was replaced by a trellis that projects horizontally in front of the water strip.

Above: Stone (set vertically so that the water flows off faster), wood, and glass form a harmonious combination of materials for the outer construction. Below: View from the southeast.

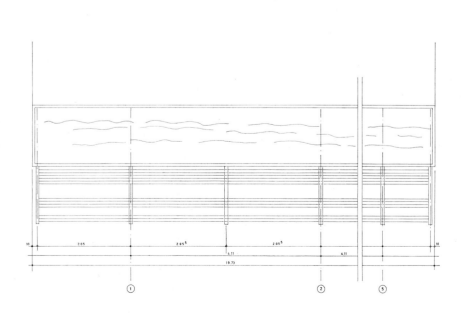

Above left: When one steps out on the balcony-terrace, the snow-covered mountains and the massively-stacked clouds drifting through the blue sky are reflected before one, as if mirrored in an Alpine lake. Below left: Here also, a water strip and projecting trellis replace a view-blocking balustrade and add the reflection of the glacier landscape to the panorama. Above: Seen from the valley over steep snowy slopes, roof and balcony lines become a not inharmonious detail in the broad general picture. Below: Not even a flight over the Alpine world would bring forth an experience of space as does this house.

Facing page, above: The view from the balcony-terrace upward to the glacier world is emphasized by the view down into the valley. A railing would have detracted from the view, and Neutra solved the problem with a reflecting water strip along the outer balcony edge. The strip is protected against freezing by hot water pipes, and the balcony-terrace floor itself is also heated, so that the snow melts in front of the broad sliding doors. Below left: Human-technical detailing strengthens the emotive power of nature through contrast. Below center: If one looks toward the southwest, the snowy mountains sink into their own shadow, as soon as the sun has disappeared behind their crestline. Below right: Double glass walls offer a transparency free of any disturbing interior distraction and allow a crystal-clear view.

Above: Night scene by the fireplace. Below left: Daytime view of the fireplace with sitting corner beyond, where intimacy is perceptibly fused with the grand vision of the glacier. Below right: Neutra's client values his fireplace especially. Night view northward toward the fireplace corner. The high windows under the tilt are shown illuminated outward, toward the northerly mountain slope.

studio also has a glass view-wall overlooking the Jungfrau chain and a window with light coming from the north. The bathroom for the studio and master bedroom is centrally placed between those two rooms.

The lower story is devoted mainly to the children's unrestricted activities and their sometimes noisy musical gatherings with other young people. The so-called jazz room, which also turns into an overnight hostel for young guests, enjoys an open fireplace. The space extends around this fireplace toward the terrace in the west and prevents one from feeling confined in a cellar when one is in this central lower-story room. Facing south and east are the children's bedrooms and the bedroom of an aunt,

Above: The intimate human scale is related to the overpowering ties of nature, even in a small guest room, through the condensed space of the diagonal roof and the space-expanding east-oriented glass front. Below: The daylight is reflected in the copper fireplace hood, with view to the left over the kitchen counter. Facing page, above left: View from the dining area to the kitchen counter. Above right: The master bedroom at the southeast corner. Below right: The laminated wood construction was executed by the carpenters of the Berner Oberland with their usual precision.

who is part of the household. Bathrooms are situated at the ends of the bedrooms. The air conditioning connects to the fireplace chimney. Also on the lower story are larders and stockrooms.

In spite of its openness to the southerly panorama, which was naturally the determining factor in the choice of the property, this Alpine house is solidly cubical and corresponds to the property lines. It evolves in steplike formation down the slope, with the view windows shaded by the projecting roof. The play of shadows, following the daily cycle, lends dynamic charm to the entire structure. Flowering shrubs sensitively enhance the entrance way and whatever is visible from the windows. Every method adopted by Neutra was used so that the design and configuration of this singular site might heighten the heart's enjoyment and invigorate the soul.

On this garden story, and reached chiefly by the main stairway from the ground floor vestibule, are guest rooms and adjoining bathrooms, each connected to the garden by spacious sliding glass doors. A southeasterly garden and patio extends in front of the guest rooms. Through a wide sliding glass door from the forecourt at the foot of this stairway, one can turn south to this garden and patio, east toward the winter garden, or north to the swimming pool. A shower and toilet are directly connected here.

Surrounding the swimming pool is a broad sun deck, which is wind-protected on the north by the house and toward the north and east by quarrystone walls. The pump house lies beneath the eastern portion of the terrace. The swimming pool itself can be subdivided during

cold weather by means of large, electric-run sliding glass walls above and a trap-door beneath the water surface to make an inside and an outside pool.

Besides the spacious furnace room, the garden story also contains a wine cellar, a maid's room, and an adjoining room for the electrical installations. These rooms are aired and lighted by shafts to the cellar. The bathrooms of the lower story make use of common plumbing.

At the top of the house, high above the living room floor, are three rooms for the household, two facing south and a third facing north. Adjoining the north room are a bath and separate toilet. Extending in front of these rooms is a small central vestibule, which receives its daylight through three plastic skylight cupolas built into the ceiling. Directly from this vestibule, one can go out onto the smaller north-roof terrace or to the large one on the south, which truly seems to overlook the world. (Food and drinks from the kitchen can be brought up by dumbwaiter to both roof terraces.) Neutra also conceived of this upper level as a water roof for insulation in summer. Mirroring the dynamic changes of color in sky and clouds, the impressive mountain chains and peaks, it provides visual and psychological links to the waters of Lago Maggiore, far below in the valley.

CASA EBELIN, BUCERIUS SOPRA NAVEGNA, SWITZERLAND

Two thousand feet above Lago Maggiore, embedded in the mountains of southern Switzerland, is the isolated site of this remarkable dwelling. The car brings the guest over a mile-long winding access road, which crosses a rushing, rocky creek in the wooded valley and climbs to the mountain-surrounded site. The visitor then climbs a short outer stairway from the north to the main entrance plat-

Above: Miles above Lago Maggiore and the surrounding mountains, with their fascinating atmospheric light changes, Neutra made careful studies for this project, which was devoted to a life-regenerative nearness to nature. Below: The architect valued the compositional significance of the northerly mountain corridor as a counterpoint for the imposing view of the mirroring lake to the south.

form. (Farther west, driving and delivery access is laid out on a steep slope down into the northerly canyon.)

The magnificent lake view, framed by tall chestnut trees and subtropical greenery, becomes visible only after one has passed the east-west spreading entrance hall into the spacious living quarters, with their wide south and east balcony terraces. As in many of this other designs, Neutra protected the rim of such high, elevated terraces by wide, shallow pools, which mirror the clouds by day and the illuminated treetops or the moonlit mountain silhouette by night. Unshackled and free of guard rails, the eye can roam here over the wide vista downward. Even from beneath and behind the fireplace—the hood of which, in part, floats suspended over the view into the landscape—the landscape is reflected in water all around the living quarters, relating intimately to the waters of the lake itself, deep and distant in the valley. The library and dining room to the west share the lake view and relate to the kitchen and service quarters to the north, which, in turn, connect with the garage to the north.

The spacious vestibule of the main

story can be separated by a door and connected to the south with the cloakroom. To the right, on the west side, is the roomy kitchen, with a sitting corner for comfortable, informal dining. From here, the owners of the house often enjoy the view of the high mountain ridges in the northeast. A dumbwaiter quickly and effortlessly moves supplies to the kitchen from the lower storerooms. The laundry room is at a side exit, near the double garage with adjoining workshop. From here, a wide stairway reaches the part of the garden story below that contains the cool storerooms.

Through a wide door adjoining the south corridor, one enters the generously proportioned living room. By means of a floor-to-ceiling glass wall, with its several sliding doors, this room is optically extended southward toward the land and lake vista. Closely related is the dining room, with its direct access to the utility area and kitchen. Adjoining the dining room, which thus lengthens the living room, is the library. Both dining room and library open to the south, with a transparent strip running the width of the room above low cupboards in front of this window-wall. Outside the living

Above: Neutra, with great interest, visited the rural stone huts of the Ticino, even those on the steepest slopes. Below: View over the steep-banked valley of the little river Navegna, southward toward the site of the modestly-silhouetted building complex. Far below, to the left, and beyond are the southerly mountain chains, which the architect wanted to underline only slightly.

Above: Northerly night view from the southwest. Center: From the southwest, the guest story with its garden terrace is only slightly visible. In the summer, the beech tree in the foreground is drawn into the composition, counterpoising its full foliage to the mountain silhouette in the background. Below: The entrance with mountain vista, which dramatizes the short ascent to the entrance platform, even when a blanket of snow replaces blossoming spring shrubs in the long planter.

room is a broad terrace. Instead of a view-blocking landing, separation to south and east is achieved by means of a wide, shallow reflecting pool in which clouds and sky are mirrored.

On the east side of the ground floor are the master bedroom, dressing room, and bath, with their water-guarded balcony over the swimming pool. From a sun deck off the bedroom and dressing room, one ascends a magnificent outer stairway for direct access to the swimming pool on the garden story, while viewing the stupendous countryside. The stairway is cantilevered from the tall walls, which protect the pool from the northern winds.

Below: Masses of masonry underline the otherwise light structure devoted to the panoramic vista. The vertical joints allow the water to run off quickly in near-freezing weather, before the cold of night causes frost damage.

A Lower floor

1 Wine cellar
2 Storage room
3 Electrical installations
4 Guest room
5 Guest room
6 Guest room
7 Patio
8 Winter garden
9 Swimming pool
10 Pool
11 Toilet

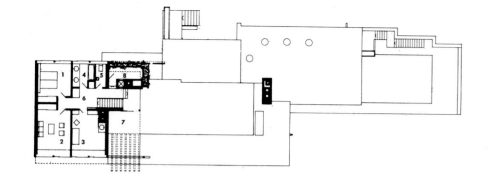

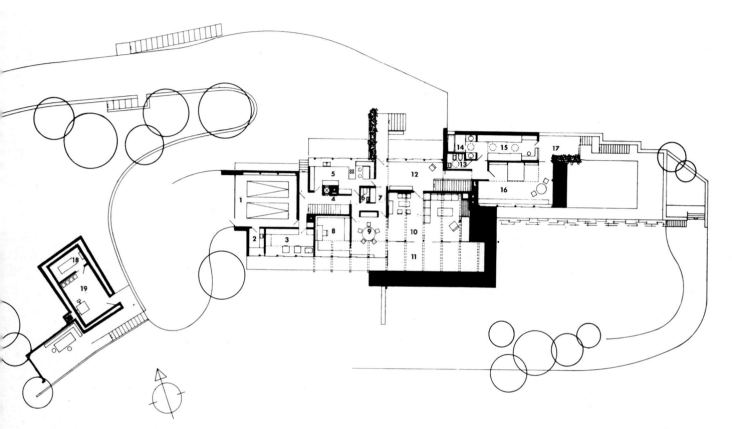

12 Shower
13 Heating and installation room
14 Gallery
15 Guest toilet
16 Guest bath
17 Guest bath
18 Pantry
19 Hall
20 Luggage room
21 Tank room

B Ground floor

1 Garage
2 Workshop
3 Washing and ironing room
4 Forecourt
5 Kitchen
6 Toilet
7 Cloakroom
8 Library
9 Dining room
10 Living room
11 Terrace

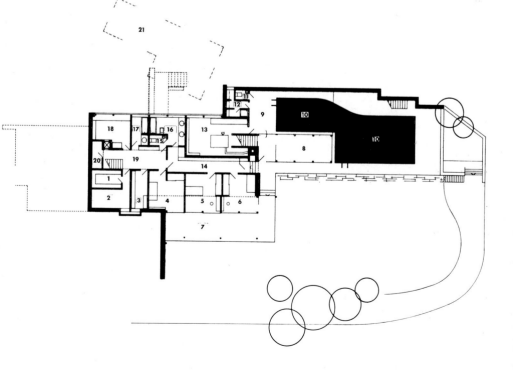

12 Hall
13 Toilet
14 Bath
15 Dressing room
16 Bedroom
17 Terrace
18 Emergency power unit
19 Refuse-burning area

C Upper floor

1 Servant's room
2 Servant's room
3 Servant's room
4 Bath
5 Toilet
6 Hall
7 Terrace
8 Terrace

Above: In all seasons, the light structure is well fitted into the massively profiled mountain landscape; even the winter scene makes the transparent view-fronts enjoyable. Below: The bedroom wing above the interior garden on a snowbound winter night; the inside pool below can be glimpsed behind the tropical plants.

Facing page, above: Night veils the back-drop of the Alpine winter landscape. Below left: When the tilt-mechanism wall under the water and the sliding door above it are opened, the outside and inside swimming pools form a superb unit, which can be glimpsed from the winter garden to the right, as well as through the interior stairway (here to the right behind the camera). Below right: Corner of the winter garden.

Above: Each step changes the play of forms in perspective. A single, fixed camera image shows too little of the experience of architecture, which, even in the midst of snow, is by no means "frozen music." Below: Stone masonry, to the left, and plate glass walls of the transparent winter garden, to the right, frame the inside pool, whose water flows freely into the much larger outside pool in the background.

Above: View over the easterly, outside swimming pool, which is temporarily separated here from the inside pool by the glass door. Below: Bathing outdoors at all seasons is an old northern custom. Empathy for the needs of the total human milieu determined Neutra's plan here in this Alpine landscape.

Facing page: Light and visual angle are of dynamic changeability, even when the extraordinary landscape milieu has receded into darkness, abstracting the architectural form somewhat and hardly enhancing it naturalistically, as by day.

Longitudinal section of swimming pool Detail

 1 Severance flap veneered in mosaic tile
 2 Caulking
 3 Pivot pin
 4 Pivot pin
 5 Bearing
 6 Bearing box
 7 Filter
 8 Electric motor
 9 Slip-clutch
10 Worm gear
11 Sprocket
12 Drive chain
13 Limit switch

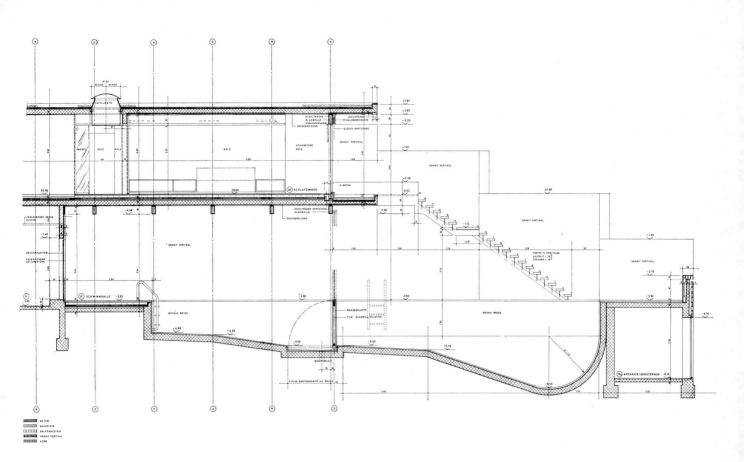

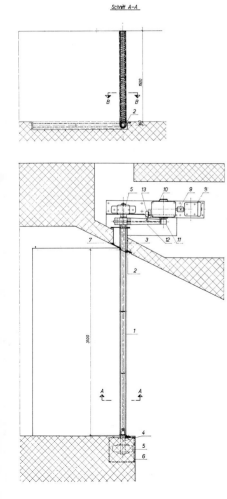

Schnitt A–A

Facing page, above left: Summer scene. The east wall of the upper story and the water mirror placed before it unite in reflecting the landscape and the distant lake. Above right: From above the master bedroom's easterly balcony water surface and the swimming pool below, one can gaze at the Alpine landscape, which changes, sometimes powerfully, sometimes subtly, with the dynamics of the seasons and the hours of the day. Below left: Winter scene. View from the northerly bath stairway and terrace into the master bedroom. Even in the bleak winter landscape, the easterly reflecting water terrace is united with the greater waters in the valley (from which the mountains rise up in the mist).

Above: In this bedroom, dawn, southerly daylight, and the indirect artificial lighting can be modulated to one's perception and suited to the hours of the day and the mood of the weather. Below: Bathroom detail.

Facing page, above: The corner fireplace by daylight. Below left: The landscape view from the living room over the terrace is unhindered by a railing. Instead, Neutra has placed a wide strip of water along the edge of the terrace, which defines the edge of the walking area. Below right: Lake landscape above the dining table.

Above: Detail of fireplace; the suspended hood permits an unrestricted view through the hearth to the landscape beyond. Below: The fireplace corner with night illumination.

Above: Transparency and reflection enhance the view of landscape and sky. Below: The terrace with its trellis often offers
an almost mystical peace by day and is
oriented toward a seemingly unpopulated
landscape.

Above: Neutra's flat roofs become mirrors for the surrounding scene, which constantly stimulates the emotions through the changing moods of the weather. Center: A guest room. Below: Another guest room, with broad plate-glass sliding doors opening toward the mountain landscape.

Above: View from the roof terrace. Below: The wide panorama individualizes every room, every terrace, especially at night.

Above: View across the roof terrace and the upper level into the westerly mountains. Below: View over the roof from the southeast; the distant skies have cleared of heavy clouds.

Left: For Neutra, union with nature was possible not only in large, spread-out, scenic places. Nature-nearness could be achieved within urban confines, as in the Research House and head office of the Neutra Institute. Here, amid the swarming traffic of Los Angeles, it is set back not quite six feet from the sidewalk of a main thoroughfare (named Silver Lake Boulevard after its adjacent central city reservoir). In this edifice, which he erected in 1932 for three households (his family and his colleagues), Neutra focused on the problem of achieving a feeling of spaciousness and privacy on a very small property of 63 × 67 feet. He planted every available piece of earth along the sidewalk and laid a little entrance bridge across a shallow reflecting pool, which lends the small property a feeling of seclusion from the urban bustle and allows the visitor to breathe somewhat more freely again before he enters.

Above: The entrant passes through a small reception room and sees in front of him the southern garden courtyard in the background; then he turns left toward the lower story or ascends the transparent stairway to the upper social rooms of the Institute. To the left, behind the gong, which summons visitors from all parts of the house to the commencement of a seminar, is one of the three bathrooms on this story, placed with ingenious accuracy, having access from both courtyards in the easterly background of this small but seemingly spacious-looking structure.

Above: From the densely planted south patio, which extends a few steps downward to the right, one sees, to the left, the stairway with a view through to the westerly greenery, while the foliage of the northerly patio beneath the planter offers the eye the pleasant goal of a distant panorama.

Right: The night-lit south patio with its light sources and installations which provide enhancing light-intensity changes. To the left, above the raised sitting area, the use of stone masonry heightens by contrast the transparency of the rest of the composition.

Facing page: The glass-enclosed balcony overlooks both garden courtyards, here in darkness.

Above: A fire in 1963 destroyed the westerly stand of protectively screening trees. The Neutra's replaced it with aluminum louvers, developed a quarter-century before and already used in the well-known Desert House. At the Los Angeles Archives building, Neutra had also erected such louvers, more than 140 feet high, on the air-conditioned glass front, behind which more than two thousand people work. These huge, slender, hollow structures, which in cross-section resemble the airfoils of jet airplanes, balance the earth's rotation automatically and follow the sun's movement in order to screen out the glare of direct rays.

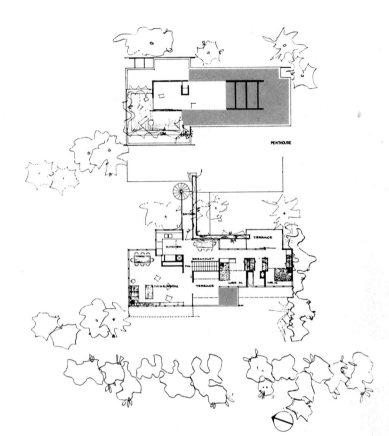

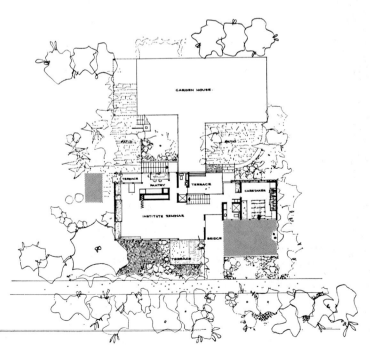

Neutra cherished the memories that relate to something set up or planted by the hand of man. Even the fallen trees, which had for so long bestowed their shadows, still arch above the entrance pool.

BIOREALISM IN THE INDIVIDUAL CASE

The single human being, the individual, according to his original, organic provenance, is never "isolated" from everything except perhaps artificially and as punishment. Even prison windows should have a view of moving evening clouds, an audible blackbird on a tree in the prison courtyard; even a morsel of such dynamics sustains life. But more of this, and also human relationships, must best be mixed into the life-diet.

From mother's womb to life's end, we are left alone wholly to ourselves for only short stretches of road, especially if we want to be happy. In emptiness, in a vacuum, no living thing feels at home, and everyone needs a world of incentives and continuous though minute stimulation. But a person feels fully happy and alive only when he himself is able to affect others in this vein. "Independent" is a word that does not really fit into natural history and into organic events. The architect has the truly wonderful vocation of seizing this in his creation, of feeling into what is individually human as well as socially satisfying, and of taking this foresight accordingly, going into a million micro-details.

His task is so fascinating precisely because it is inexhaustible, and he seeks ever more refined solutions that do justice to our senses—many more than just five—and trillions of nervous reactions, night and day, and during growth and aging. This task of the architect will easily fill a long future, far beyond all passing fashions of the day. We recognize here a truly lasting, life-supporting program.

Naturally, the molder of our milieu must first become familiar with present-day, fast-improving research, with the deeper insights into psychosomatics, into the fundamentals of body-and-soul relationships, and thus precisely with life itself. Toward this he aims with his empathy and his arrangement of inciting stimuli for eyes, ears, touch, the feeling for warmth and cold, and everything else in our manifold and yet-so-interlocking sensual endowment, which is often involved truly on many levels, even in the subconscious.

I was always delighted when I could anticipate just this subconscious. Clients became personally very close to me and developed into the best of friends precisely during the building of a single dwelling, and then would sincerely affirm that I had truly attained such correct anticipations and satisfactions.

All this cannot really be seen in pictures. Neither the art of photography nor the motion picture is sufficient here. Architecture, its interior and exterior, must ever anew come to us in so many sensual impressions, probed and fused. Thus, one must "actually experience it," as people did in earlier times, before they judged with preconceptions. That was before the invention of our picture-magazine civilization, where one usually thinks one knows about so much more from all over and yet has so much less "through-and-through" first-hand knowledge.

The most modern biological science, as represented by my honored friends René Dubos of the Rockefeller Institute or the Nobel prize winner Roger Williams of Texas, doubts simplified statements about "averages" and "the average." In life matters, it is dangerously confusing to speak of the important as if it were average.

Now the "single dwelling" is the task that always trains us architects to look with very consequential attention precisely into what is the innately individual. Sincere attention to the innate and to that which is life-conditioned differently in every single person cannot simply fall under the drawing board, even if, pressed by need, we often prepare to settle thousands and bring them, young and old, into a reciprocal life relationship. The whole natural history of evolution would be frozen solid and finally at its benumbed end if there were no individual divergencies, mutations, deviations—of which always a few turn out to be at least surprisingly fitted for a long life span. And from there, from such minute examples, effective evolution proceeds.

Our habitat—and especially the settling of people in the many landscapes of our globe, perhaps soon of our planetary system—should be a truly life-supporting arrangement and a happily assertive union with the environment, and it should still be able to show the importance of the family unit with conviction. This is a very old anthropological matter which the architect seems destined to support with the most modern means and materials and, above all, with new understanding.

To become rooted is a basic organic fact; to anchor oneself is a human necessity. Also, a repetitive pattern of movement, the setting down of accommodating and life-serving routes—be it for birds of passage, migratory fish, or the emotional homecoming of people in city bumper-to-bumper traffic—belong to a degree to the impressive, formative, self-regenerating story of creation.

For the world of building of today, there is also the fast expansion into all climes, the unique unaccustomed spreading-out over the developing countries, where billions queue up to buy our civilization. All here depends on the planners, who first have trained heart and mind precisely in the individual case, in order also to responsibly quicken their artistic initiative, believing in the necessary scientific penetration into "the problem of man"—an individual functioning within ecology, which vitally keeps and supports him.

We must set to work a new, true-to-life humanism, which is by no means separated from the much older one relating to natural history—rather strengthened by it and fructified a thousandfold.

RESTLESSNESS AND TRANQUIL SECURITY

There is a basic problem that must occupy the architect especially. Our life is borne by a subconscious remembrance, an emotional, sensual knowledge of security. This quite irrational "having experienced" stems from our first habitation, our previous life in the mother's womb, which is so mysteriously protected by nature. There were no engineering or air-conditioning problems to solve there! As in no earthly dwelling place thereafter, we swayed softly and surely there, in a warm, biologically wonderful and complete individual security, in which we felt so good that we began only slowly, yet increasingly, to desire movement.

Only with the beginning of growth in the outside world, with the attempt to crawl over the ground and its impediments, does something like a shadow of rational thinking begin. But it is not this alone that finally brings us to our feet and later to automobile tires and that thrusts us on through life. It is the even-more-complex dynamism of the brain, which is a true driving mechanism more powerful even than rational mechanics.

Behind our brain and the anterior lobe with its logic, lies the much older and therefore much more powerful mid-brain, in which all our thinking is continually being moved minutely or heftily moved by emotions, making us truly restless. Emotions are the actual drive for our "endogenous" restlessness, which a mother comes to feel in the last months of carrying her child.

Therefore, we had better not speak too much of rational reasons for uprootedness. Rootedness, which certainly is fundamental, is also poled against something else. For all their restlessness, therefore, the Americans have quite primeval aspects as a base—they have all of humanity as ancestors. And the whole animal kingdom is their ancestry as well.

When I submitted my book "Wie baut Amerika?" ("How American Builds") to the publishers in 1925, I used an overpoweringly beautiful image by my friend Edward Weston, the great photographer, as the first illustration. It depicted the impressive tent of the typical American traveling circus which is as characteristic for North America as the teepee of the Indian nomads, who followed the wild buffalo herds as their hunting booty. But, from time immemorial, some human beings—even more than other, less brainy animals—have been "unnecessarily" restless and have, accordingly, often been critically judged by their more conservative fellows.

Prehistoric streets have been found and researched by anthropologists. The exchange of modes of behavior and of "goods" was apparently always very exciting and went beyond the merely practical. At least a few individuals always reacted against pale conservatism, looked around for something different, and thereby mobilized at least a small following. From Aachen, which thousands of years later was the burial place of Charlemagne, a curious, much-traveled traffic route ran eastward into the Urals. Also long ago, a trading and traffic route extended from the Baltic Sea southward and straight through Europe, winding its way over the most treacherous Alpine passes to Genoa, the city which, many thousands of years later, became the birthplace of Christopher Columbus, who was to sail with his assorted crew to America.

Thus, on the huge American continent, Indian tribes hunted buffalo and battled with each other until they were shut up in reserves. My son Raymond has worked with these now very unfortunately settled reserve residents as an untiring doctor and medical anthropologist.

When I had to deal with the preparatory planning of the Atatürk University in Erzurum, I observed with wonder how the Kurds, still today, drive six million cattle from south to north and back again through all of Anatolia, in search of pastureland for every season. Thus, nomadic life has all possible basis as a living pattern, on the surface, and, as suggested, probably is deeply rooted within our long evolutionary past.

Professor Freud, whom I knew as a very young man and as his sons' friend within his own remarkable family circle, discovered without going much into the physical environment, a certain "discomfort in culture." Culture sometimes seems like a solidly walled-up dungeon with prisoners inside. Karl Lorenz, that keen observer and animal psychologist, does indeed speak of a "reflex of eruption" in animals as well. It was interesting for me to discuss this with him as an architect. No organism wants to be locked in or would shut itself off from the exterior dynamics of nature, except, for instance, on occasion, for short regenerative periods, when it may or can draw the curtain before the panorama of the world.

Thus it is no wonder, be it in Detroit or Wolfsburg or wherever exports go from there, that everyone who has even the smallest car steps on the gas and moves off faster and for greater distances than the average Phoenician or Portuguese ever did with their toilsome rudders or sailboats, in the age-old bent for exploration.

And yet, when all this has been said and admitted, the need for anchorage seems to be an even more profound, biologically primeval reflex. Rootedness is a means toward development and bears fundamental healing powers. It nourishes us quite basically, psychosomatically speaking.

The architect and the city planner, whose work is directed toward fulfilling this deeply powerful wish of man for his own place on earth, can in one way or another check excessive restlessness and can so make today's loud and restless melting pot cease to seethe and make it quietly crystallize.

It will not be just spacemen who will in the end be encapsulated in interesting transparency. Ordinary earth dwellers can also daily be regenerated explorers as they look through large clear thermopane glass at windswept tree-tops under morning clouds.

But especially the architect and the city planner themselves must now go wandering and discovering together with their assistants. Today their services are used world over, and a far-reaching measure for values is used. The regional, however we evaluate it, is as little their domain as it is for violinists and conductors of music, who are engaged from Berlin to Buenos Aires and perform a symphony together in the festivals of Salzburg, Lucerne, or Edinburgh.

A world-wide criterion exists here, as in the building of airports, hospitals, and internal hostelries. The Hilton hotels in West Berlin, Cairo, Karachi, or Caracas are projects closely resembling that of the Rila Hotel in Sofia. That seems to be the pace the world sets, and it did not start just yesterday.

But even if the purely technical side of the VW, Volvo, or Ford variant differs as little in manufacturing methods as in mass consumption itself, the matter of an enduring habitat is something else again. Here more subtly complex activities and functions come into play. And these are often "conditioned" for a long time and in varying degrees. However, such influences are scarcely on the upswing anymore, and this seems to be a certain fact.

The prototype of such a lifetime dwelling is the single house, and it is perhaps of prime importance to the student of architecture as it shelters and protects man and, having been his home since primeval times, conditions his earliest memories.

The separate dwelling and the living unit that serve a family of old and young over many years of organic growth and interaction are human biological tasks of the first order, and all the patented technology or economy of rapid assembly will be of no avail if requirements of the body and soul are filled in a miserable and insufficient manner. For a long time now, I have called this the sole realism, which retains its validity beyond the period of amortization.

Bank debts can be amortized in time. What we owe organic nature cannot be eradicated for all eternity, and we are bound to it not by the month but for every life-second.

The Neutra Institute in America and Europe, which its founders have most kindly and aspiringly named after my strivings of half a century, has made from this honest pioneering work the significant continually deepening idea of "biorealism" its program and its goal, for the benefit of the inhabitant, man, woman, and child.

Life-realism, biorealism, yearly fed by so many scientific research papers, is a new and growing humanism. Withering away and sickness, pathology—for this, the individual and a people have to pay most dearly. The architect is a physiotherapist and an economist; he can certainly support vitality and health, without which each individual life and each living in togetherness becomes depraved.*

Only that which is built close to nature is in the minutest detail life-sustaining. And for the naked eye, the visible union with the landscape becomes a tangible, encouraging symbol.

* As early as 1927, Richard Neutra tried to place his Health House close to nature, like a bird's nest nestling into the landscape; all his other houses are its successors in their efforts to be "nature-near."

ACKNOWLEDGMENTS

It is in keeping with Richard Neutra and the Richard Neutra Institute in Europe and America, symbolically named after Neutra's lifelong pioneering work by its founders who are dedicated to a better environment, that, as in earlier publications, grateful tribute is paid to those co-workers, partners, and colleagues who helpfully participated in this significant work. The books about Neutra's buildings and projects published in Switzerland by Verlag Girsberger and Verlag für Architektur (Artemis) provide, as Neutra had always wished, a more complete list, spanning the years, of all those who joined him in his work. Lack of space restricts us to the following incomplete list: Robert Alexander; Ramberg & Lowrey; Dan Rowland; Karl Heinz Rebstock, Hamburg; Gustav Luettge, Erich Schneider-Wessling, Cologne; Roland Weber, Düsseldorf; M. Mittag, Wuppertal; Harold H. Le Roith, Johannesburg; Christian Trippl, Chur; Bruno Honegger, Zurich; Gert Offermann, Wuppertal; Hans Hochgesand, Mainz; and, for many years, Thaddeus Longstreth, Princeton.

While they accomplished much in their own right and did so joyfully, Benno Fischer, Serge Koschin, John Blanton, Egon Winkens, Hans von Escher, Gunnar Serneblad, Perry Neuschatz, Gert and Ute Lehmann, Augusto Lodi, Jack Kellner, Toby Schmidbauer, Herbert Weisskamp, and, from the earliest period, Gregory Ain and Harwell Harris, as well as other young men esteemed by Richard and Dion Neutra, may have taken with them, from the residences shown here, beneficial stimulation to last a lifetime.

Dion Neutra, who ever since the 1942 Channel Heights housing project has collaborated in many father-and-son projects, was for years a partner and now is manager of the office of Richard and Dion Neutra, Architects & Associates.

For half a century, Mrs. Dione Neutra was her husband's most constant collaborator; and her truly deep interest in the philosophy of a bioreal molding of our human milieu and in the goals of the Institute devolved upon its advisers as well as on her sons, the architect Dion Neutra and the doctor and medical anthropologist Raymond Neutra.

The charming sketches of Bewobau Walldorf project were done by Gerfried Ramsauer of Vienna.

Grateful thanks are expressed to the photographers whose pictures are reproduced here— especially Neutra's collaborator of a decade, Julius Shulman, of Los Angeles; Amin Farr; the late Martin Hesse, of Bern; Lawrence S. Williams, of Pennsylvania; Juerg Bay, of Zurich; Fritz Rentsch, Jr., of Paris; Alberto Flammer, of Ticino; and Schmölz-Huth, of Cologne.